Anti-Fraud Risk and Control Workbook

PETER GOLDMANN

WILEY

JOHN WILEY & SONS, INC.

Published by John Wiley & Sons, Inc., Hoboken, New Jersey.
Published simultaneously in Canada.

For general information on our other products and services or for technical support, please contact our Customer
Care Department within the United States at (800) 762-2974, outside the United States at (317) 572-3993 or fax
(317) 572-4002.

Wiley also publishes its books in a variety of electronic formats. Some content that appears in print may not be
available in electronic books. For more information about Wiley products, visit our web site at www.wiley.com.

Library of Congress Cataloging-in-Publication Data:

Goldmann, Peter, 1953-
    Anti-fraud audit and control workbook / Peter Goldmann.
        p.   cm.
    Includes bibliographical references and index.
    ISBN 978-0-470-49653-4 (pbk.)
        1. Fraud—United States—Case studies. 2. Fraud—United States—Prevention. 3. Auditing. 4. Forensic accounting.
I. Title.
    HV6695.G585   2009
    658.4'73—dc22

                                                                                2009015536

Printed in the United States of America

10   9   8   7   6   5   4   3   2   1

Contents

Preface

"Few people begin their careers with the goal of becoming liars, cheats, and thieves. Yet that turns out to be the destiny of all too many."

—Joseph T. Wells, Founder and Chairman,
Association of Certified Fraud Examiners

This quote says it all when we refer to the perpetrators of fraud. The world's great anti-fraud guru, Joe Wells, teaches us the critical reality that most people are either honest or want to be. They don't, as Wells points out, set out to be career fraudsters.

The problem is that life's inevitable curveballs sometimes are all it takes to push a fundamentally moral, honest individual to cross the line from integrity to crime. The *Anti-Fraud Risk and Control Workbook* is designed to give internal auditors, accountants, and other financial professionals in all organizations a foundation of practical knowledge about the fraud that can impact their organizations.

This book appears at a time when the need for awareness about the mechanics of major types of internal and external fraud and the red flags that raise suspicion is more acute than in recent memory. For years, the incidence of fraud has been steadily increasing and along with it, the number of dollars lost to these crimes. And while this is clear evidence that fraud flourishes during periods of economic growth and prosperity, it virtually explodes when the economy turns south.

Naturally, we all hope that the recession that commenced in 2007—or any future recession for that matter—won't motivate too many fundamentally honest people to add further credence to Joe Wells's apt observation. However, regardless of the economy's vicissitudes in coming months and years, history proves that the "fraud problem" will undoubtedly worsen. The key for management is to acknowledge this, raise the task of fraud risk mitigation much higher on the organization's priority list, and allocate the human and financial resources necessary to at least eliminate as many of the identifiable fraud risks threatening it now and in the future.

The following pages are the product of several years of research and writing about ways to battle the seemingly relentless assault on institutions of all kinds by fraudsters of all kinds. It is hoped that some of the many fraud-fighting tools from the contents of this book will assist dedicated managers in safeguarding their organizations' reputations and assets.

—Peter Goldmann, June 2009

▶ A Short History of Fraud

Fraud against organizations of all kinds has been around forever. However, with the rapid growth of Western capitalism in the 19th and 20th centuries, the temptations for employees *and* outsiders to steal from the increasingly numerous institutions spawned by the explosive success of free market commerce began to spread.

Even seemingly honest employees and outsiders, such as vendors or customers, found themselves increasingly tempted to exploit opportunities in the financial and operational functions of corporations, banks, government agencies, and non-profit organizations to enrich themselves illegally.

By the early 1920s, Western financial markets had become relatively modern. They had fueled the capitalization and rapid growth of major industries such as automobiles, broadcasting, construction and oil, transportation and chemicals.

However, along with the industrial race to technological modernization and the huge fortunes amassed by investment banks, their corporate clients, and the wealthy individuals who traded stocks and bonds, came rampant greed on the part of the "haves," while America's "have-nots," whose ranks swelled through the devastation of the Great Depression, became increasingly motivated to defraud "the system."

The boom ended with a disastrous bust starting on October 29, 1929 when Wall Street experienced its *first* bona fide crisis. Not long after that—1933 to be exact—the world's first major anti-fraud legislation was passed. The genesis of the Securities Act of 1933 was nicely summarized by Deepa Sarkar while a student at the Securities Law Clinic at Cornell University Law School:

> In the period leading up to the stock market crash, companies issued stock and enthusiastically promoted the value of their company to induce investors to purchase those securities. Brokers in turn sold this stock to investors based on promises of large profits but with little disclosure of other relevant information about the company. In many cases, the promises made by companies and brokers had little or no substantive basis, or were wholly fraudulent. With thousands of investors buying up stock in hopes of huge profits, the market was in a state of speculative frenzy that only ended . . . when the market crashed as panicky investors sold off their investments *en masse*.
>
> In reaction to this calamity, and at President Franklin Roosevelt's instigation, Congress set out to enact laws that would prevent speculative frenzies. After a series of hearings that brought to light the severity of the abuses leading to the crash, Congress enacted the Securities Act of 1933.[1]

Unfortunately, while the "'33 Act," as it was often called, did significantly reduce insider trading, phony securities schemes, and other investment scams, it failed to address the problem of corporate financial fraud involving "cooking the books" by manipulating sales, earnings, and other financial results, and perpetrating other schemes that either misled the investing public *or* illegally enriched the top executives who ran these companies—or both.

In 1985, in response to widespread U.S. campaign finance fraud and overseas bribery, the Committee of Sponsoring Organizations (COSO) of the Treadway Commission was formed. Its mandate: To develop accounting rules and procedures to prevent the increasingly widespread practice of illegal financial reporting. COSO was initially sponsored by five major U.S. financial organizations:

- American Institute of Certified Public Accountants (AICPA)
- American Accounting Association (AAA)
- Financial Executives Institute (FEI)
- Institute of Internal Auditors (IIA)
- Institute of Management Accountants (IMA)

COSO came up with the original concept of "Internal Controls" with regard to corporate financial reporting. It published a set of guidelines to assist accountants and auditors to ensure that their organizations did not fall victim to the illegal ways of dishonest financial executives, top managers, and accountants.

Despite its noble intentions, the so-called COSO Framework did not stop large U.S. corporations from abusing the trust of their boards and shareholders, not to mention the loopholes in accounting laws and rules.

The result. Enron, Tyco, Worldcom, Adelphia, and a now well-known string of other massive corporate financial scandals of the late 1990s and early 2000s. This prompted Congress to take another shot at devising legislation that would restore public confidence in the U.S. capital markets and erect substantive regulatory deterrents to future large-scale white-collar crimes. The result was the Sarbanes-Oxley Act of July 2, 2002. This Act—widely referred to as "SOX"—laid the groundwork for a world standard for the integrity of publicly reported financial information.

SOX contains stringent financial reporting rules and penalties for noncompliance for corporate boards, executives, directors, auditors, attorneys, and securities analysts. Advocates touted the new law as powerful action that would at long last protect the investing public. Skeptics, by contrast, argued from the beginning of the SOX debate that implementing such a law would not make the problem of fraudulent financial reporting go away.

Regrettably, the latter were right. While the United States has not sustained a fraud-fueled corporate implosion of Enron proportions since SOX came into effect in 2002, statistics show that institutional fraud has *not* been deterred. On the contrary, as you'll see in the next section, fraud has actually skyrocketed in recent years.

The same applies internationally. Scandals at Germany's Siemens AG, Italy's Parmalat, South Korea's Daewoo, numerous Russian financial institutions, and Chinese manufacturers prove that international regulations for financial management, auditing, and reporting are desperately needed.

A promising milestone was reached in 2002 when the U.S. accounting industry implemented *Statement on Auditing Standards #99 (SAS 99)* which placed unprecedented responsibility on auditors for detecting fraud in organizations' financial records. Much of the rest of the world followed suit in 2003. And in 2004, the International Federation of Accountants (IFAC) completed work on International Standard on Auditing (ISA) #240, a virtual mirror-image of *SAS 99*.

The result. With IFAC's 123 member countries now committed to audit standards specifically designed to screen for fraud, most of the world's auditors now have clear guidelines for detecting fraudulent financial activity in their clients' financial records.

Important. While *SAS 99* and ISA 240 are directed principally at external auditors, the Institute of Internal Auditors (IIA) has strongly endorsed the fraud-auditing methods and procedures contained in these critical standards for all internal professionals in a position to detect fraud.

The question for investors, customers, vendors, and managers now is whether the global financial and economic meltdown of 2008–2009 will render the new laws, regulations, and audit guidelines impotent in the face of the inevitable increase in pressure to cook the books, embezzle funds, and commit a variety of other frauds that come along with all major economic downturns.

Most anti-fraud experts concur that no matter how well-written the rules may be, institutional fraud will *always* spike upward when economic and financial markets are slumping. It can only be hoped that history will show the Great Global Meltdown of 2008–2009 to have passed *without* the heavy fraud-generated corporate casualties that many doomsayers had predicted leading up to the crisis.

▶ About This Book

The *Anti-Fraud Risk and Control Workbook* is not industry-specific, and therefore of value to professionals in *all* corporate, not-for-profit, and government entities. Other workbooks in this series address specific industries such as financial services, healthcare, and not-for-profit.

Chapter 1 gives you a sense of just how extensive and costly the current fraud "problem" is with an array of key statistics. Chapters 2–5 delve into the two main types of fraud—internal and external—including the important differences between frauds committed by employees and those committed by their superiors in senior and executive management positions. The remaining chapters (6–8) provide detailed advice on how to detect and prevent fraud in your organization.

All of the workbooks in this series aim to engage readers in an easy-to-follow combination of instructional text and interactive exercises. The *Anti-Fraud Risk and Control Workbook* includes:

- Sixteen case studies of actual frauds, included to help illustrate key points in the chapter. Each case study includes an overview of how it happened, a recap of the key points, and the question "How Could This Have Been Prevented?" List as many preventive measures as you can, and then check your answers against the ones found in Appendix B. As you progress through the Workbook, your list of measures will grow as you become more knowledgeable about the dynamics of how fraud is committed, detected, and prevented.

- End-of-chapter quizzes to help you test your newfound knowledge. Answer as many questions as you can and then check them against the answer key found in Appendix A. These quizzes contain no trick questions; they are standard-format questions to help you complete the Workbook, earn your CPE credits, and—most importantly—help you fight fraud and corruption at your organization.

Remember

Throughout this Workbook, you will see boxes titled "Remember." These are flags for key facts, concepts or topics to pay particular attention to as you build your knowledge about fraud.

▶ About White-Collar Crime 101 LLC

White-Collar Crime 101 LLC (WCC 101) was founded in 1998 in Connecticut by Peter Goldmann, a graduate of the London School of Economics, and an established business journalist who had reported and edited many domestic and international business publications.

The company came into being as the result of Mr. Goldmann's acquisition of a monthly newsletter called *White-Collar Crime Fighter* directed primarily at law enforcement personnel.

After acquiring the publication, Mr. Goldmann redesigned it and reformulated its purpose and content, thus establishing it as the only monthly subscription-based publication designed to provide useful, actionable, anti-fraud advice and insight to the private sector.

Over the following years, *White-Collar Crime Fighter* published articles based on interviews and contributions from hundreds of top U.S. and overseas anti-fraud experts from the fields of auditing, accounting, law, investigation, forensics, finance, compliance, and regulation.

Today, the publication enjoys a reputation as a leading source of reliable "how-to" information on detecting, preventing, investigating, and prosecuting fraud.

Thanks to *White-Collar Crime Fighter's* success, several subscribers approached WCC 101 asking if the company provided employee fraud awareness training. At the time, around 2001, the answer was no. However, Mr. Goldmann wondered why large corporations were coming to his publication for training. It must have meant, he reasoned, that no one else was offering such training, which to him seemed like a basic anti-fraud imperative for any organization, given the already serious and continuously growing threat of fraud.

After some digging, the WCC 101 team determined that indeed, there was no such "employee-friendly" anti-fraud training on the market. There was plenty of training for "the profession"—for fraud examiners, accountants, auditors, and law enforcement investigators; but nothing that taught employees how to recognize the red flags of fraudulent conduct in their organizations or how to report such incidents if they were detected.

Long story short, Mr. Goldmann resolved to fill this gap in the market for anti-fraud tools. He conceived and developed *FraudAware*, a customizable Web-based ("E-Learning") fraud awareness course designed for large companies. The basic, "generic" *FraudAware* program was completed in mid-2002—just around the time when Congress was dotting the "i's" and crossing the "t's" of the Sarbanes Oxley Act.

As executives of public companies (*FraudAware's* initial targeted market) quickly learned that SOX compliance was going to cost them multiple millions of dollars and countless hours from the schedules of their internal auditors, accountants, senior financial executives, and attorneys, employee fraud awareness training was a decidedly low priority.

By 2005, as the financial and human resources burdens of SOX compliance had begun to decline, management at many organizations began to realize that despite its massive investments in SOX compliance, the problem was not getting better, in fact it was getting worse.

The result. A growing number of organizations began to realize that they had to mobilize their greatest asset—their employees—to actively assist in the fight against fraud.

FraudAware training became a logical tool for accomplishing this, and indeed in recent years, the team of *FraudAware* subject matter experts, instructional designers, and E-Learning "techies" has been extremely busy, implementing customized training courses at organizations in all major industries in the United States and overseas.

Today, WCC 101 is the premier provider of published anti-fraud information and maintains the largest searchable Web-based archive of practical actionable fraud prevention information. It also has a reputation of being the only provider of customized anti-fraud training designed, developed, and implemented by a team of top SME's *and* instructional professionals.

With the publication of *The Anti-Fraud Risk and Control Workbook*, WCC 101 adds another valuable source of practical anti-fraud training and guidance.

Acknowledgments

This workbook would not have been possible without the generous support and assistance of the following thought leaders in fraud prevention, detection, and investigation:

- Stephen Pedneault, CPA, CFE, Forensic Accounting Services, LLC
- Jeffrey Rossi, CPA, CFE, J.H. Cohn, LLP
- Christine Doxey, CAPP, CCS, Vice President of Business Development, Business Strategy Inc.

Thanks also to the many anti-fraud experts who generously shared their time to be interviewed for articles published in *White-Collar Crime Fighter* thereby enabling me to acquire valuable new knowledge for this project.

Appreciation also goes to John Wiley & Sons for choosing to add this new workbook format to its impressive array of anti-fraud titles.

Why No Organization Is Immune to Fraud

Did you know that:

- Organizations lose an average of 7 percent of gross revenue to fraud every year? In 2008 that represented approximately $994 billion.[1]

- The most common method by which fraud is detected is tips? Over 46 percent of cases that are detected are reported via a tip from an employee, vendor, or other whistle-blower.[2]

- Fraudulent financial reporting—the main form of management fraud, is twice as common in organizations as billing schemes—the most common form of employee-level fraud?[3]

- Organizations that implement entity-wide fraud awareness training cut fraud losses by 52 percent?[4]

- Seventy-four percent of employees report that they have observed or have firsthand knowledge of wrongdoing in their organization in the past 12 months?[5]

- The average fraudulent financial reporting fraud costs the victim organization $2 million, while the average loss per incident of billing fraud is only $100,000?[6]

- The majority of public companies investigated by the Securities and Exchange Commission (SEC) for fraud subsequently suffer a substantial decline in stock price (50 percent or more)?[7]

- It takes an average of 24 months for a fraud to be detected?[8]

- One-third of large-organization executives say they have no documented investigative policies or procedures for fraud, and one-half have no incident response plan?[9]

- One-quarter of companies consider themselves *highly vulnerable* to information theft, and 29 percent have experienced information theft, loss, or attack in the past three years?[10]

- The most common type of fraud affecting institutions, by far, is theft of assets—which can include money, services, or physical assets?[11]

Chapter 1 introduces the critical notion that you as a financial professional have considerable power to prevent, detect, and report fraud. The chapter also covers the following topics:

- The multiple definitions of fraud that make it critical to clarify the *real* meaning of the term in your mind
- A number of widespread myths about fraud and the realities that they misinterpret
- Management's role as the standard setter for an ethical and law-abiding institutional culture

It is not possible to compile a workbook on fraud fighting without relying to a considerable degree on the prodigious and wide-ranging research conducted by the Association of Certified Fraud Examiners (ACFE). However, in addition to this authoritative body, founded in 1988 in Austin, Texas, by Joseph T. Wells, the Big Daddy of the anti-fraud profession, there are other respected institutions whose research provides additional useful material for the study of institutional fraud.

As with the list of statistics that open the chapter, the following pages draw on key findings of numerous prominent consulting, research, and academic institutions that are active in supporting the fight against fraud in organizations of all kinds—corporations, both public and private, not-for-profit organizations, and governmental agencies. These carefully selected statistics provide a framework defining the vast scope of the fraud problem. With the perspective provided by these data, you will be equipped with a solid understanding of the magnitude of the fraud problem, along with key trends and patterns in major categories of fraud.

▶ What Is Fraud?

Most people involved in the fraud-fighting business have their own concept of what fraud is—and what it isn't. As a result we have a grab bag of definitions to choose from in guiding our day-to-day work. Some are legal definitions. Others are academic, while still others are based on personal experience. Out of the lot, the most useful definitions boil down to two.

According to the ACFE, fraud is:

> Any illegal acts characterized by deceit, concealment, or violation of trust. These acts are not dependent upon the application of threat of violence or of physical force. Frauds are perpetrated by individuals and organizations to obtain money, property, or services; to avoid payment or loss of services; or to secure personal or business advantage.[12]

According to the American Institute of Certified Public Accountants (AICPA), fraud is:

> A broad legal concept that is distinguished from error depending on whether the action is intentional or unintentional.[13]

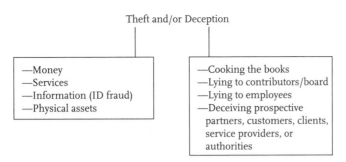

Theft and/or Deception

—Money
—Services
—Information (ID fraud)
—Physical assets

—Cooking the books
—Lying to contributors/board
—Lying to employees
—Deceiving prospective
 partners, customers, clients,
 service providers, or
 authorities

Exhibit 1.1   White-Collar Crime 101 Definition

The bottom line. Regardless of whose definition of fraud you accept, you will find that nearly all incidents of fraudulent activity—also called white-collar crime—fall into one or both of two categories: Theft and Deception. Exhibit 1.1 is a graphic illustration of this dual-category definition of fraud, as formulated by White-Collar Crime 101.

▶ Myths and Realities about Fraud

One of the key reasons for the astounding breadth and depth of the fraud problem is that management often operates under the false impression that its organization is immune to fraud.

More precisely, top executives like to think that because they have complied with rules and laws requiring them to put internal controls in place, they are adequately protected against attacks by white-collar criminals. In reality, *no* organization—no matter how well-designed its internal controls against fraud are—can ever be fully protected against determined fraudsters. The bad guys always find loopholes or weaknesses in your operations that they can exploit to steal cash, forge checks, collude with vendors, falsify financial reports, steal confidential data, or commit any of a million other crimes that cause either financial or reputational damage—or both.

In addition to this false sense of self-protection, other common yet potentially costly misconceptions that senior managers often have about fraud are illustrated in the following myths.

■ Myth #1: Ethics and Compliance Training "Has Us Covered"

This myth assumes that such training addresses key issues about fraud and instructs employees how to detect the red flags of fraud and how to report it. See Exhibit 1.2.

In fact, compliance and ethics typically have little to do with fraud. Nearly all organizations have a code of ethics on which this training is based. However the vast majority of such codes don't even contain the word "fraud."

In most organizations, such a code informs employees about issues like sexual harassment, antitrust issues, accepting gifts from vendors, and other ethical matters that are important—but are not related to fraud.

The important thing to remember is that while all fraud is unethical, not all unethical conduct is fraudulent. For example, accepting a generous gift from a

Exhibit 1.2   Fraud Training versus Ethics Training

vendor—such as a free vacation, tickets to professional sporting events, or other such items—is unethical and most likely in direct violation of your organization's ethics policy. However, such gifts are *not* necessarily illegal, and hence they often do not represent fraud.

■ Myth #2: Our Finance Staff Are Qualified to Protect Us Against Fraud

This notion is equally misconceived. Internal auditors, financial managers, accountants, treasurers, and other professionals in most organizations are usually *untrained* in fraud detection and prevention, and they most certainly are not trained—let alone expected—to be fraud investigators. However, in many organizations, there is growing pressure for internal auditors and other financial managers to focus more on fraud detection—which may be one reason you are reading this book!

■ Myth #3: We Have Very Little Fraud Here

The problem arises when this assumption is made without firm quantitative proof. In too many organizations, senior management believes there is little fraud because management *wants* to believe that. In the meantime, employees, vendors, or customers could be stealing huge amounts of money.

One of the most stunning examples of the "we-have-no-fraud-here" myth is the case of subprime mortgage fraud. Banks were lending money to unqualified mortgage borrowers by the billions in the 1990s and leading up to the housing crash that began in early 2007. Because housing prices were on a historic upward trend, top executives at large mortgage lenders were making money hand over fist as their sales people, underwriters, and independent mortgage brokers essentially threw every standard for loan qualification out the window, confident that if a borrower ultimately proved unable to make the monthly payments, the bank could foreclose and sell the property at a profit.

What the bankers failed to address was the question of how much fraud was being perpetrated by brokers, appraisers, attorneys, and even their own underwriters in order to meet increasingly challenging quotas for loan closings.

The truth was that throughout the country, lenders were approving more and more so-called liar's loans, a colloquialism for "stated income" loans—which are approved by lenders without checking tax returns, employment history, credit history, or any other pertinent financial background on the applicant. Moreover, leading up to the subprime crisis, prospective borrowers were virtually *encouraged* by mortgage brokers to defraud lenders by filling out mortgage applications with completely fictitious income figures and making up numbers reflecting their assets and liabilities and so forth. But to shareholders, regulators, and the general public, bank executives claimed that their lending operations where completely professional and that no fraud was involved.

The truth only came out after the crash—when regulators, lenders' attorneys, and politicians started digging into the matter and discovered that as much as 90 percent of stated income loans were made despite at least *some* fraudulent application or tax return information.[14]

This example is only one of many that you could find to debunk the "no fraud here" myth that many senior executives *throughout* the U.S. business community continue to embrace.

In reality, *no* organization is immune to fraud. Some organizations have less than others. But anyone in the anti-fraud profession will tell you that if a company, not-for-profit, or government agency says they have no fraud, they are either outright lying or hopelessly naïve.

■ Myth #4: Fraud Is a Necessary Cost of Doing Business

Really? Can you imagine what the tens of thousands of former employees of Enron, WorldCom, Adelphia, Bear Stearns, and others would say to that?

You may say, "A large organization can afford a bit of fraud because they are financially sound, and it may cost more to catch the fraudsters than to write off the losses."

The problem with this reasoning is that when the fraudsters know that you do not take action against "small frauds," or educate their workforce about fraud, they are encouraged to attempt larger ones. If the organization has no firm policy for investigating and punishing known fraudsters, it is actually inviting dishonest people to steal. The eventual result will be that so-called small frauds eventually accumulate into major losses. And when that occurs and the news media find out about it, the reputational damage to the organization can be serious enough to drive away customers and incur scrutiny of government authorities that could seriously endanger the organization's financial health.

■ Myth #5: Implementing Controls and Training Is Costly

In reality, fraud losses are much costlier. If, as the ACFE has determined, your organization loses up to 7 percent of its revenue to fraud every year, you can do the math to calculate approximately how many actual dollars are lost to fraud each year. Even if the ACFE is off by, say, 25 percent for the sake of argument, your organization's fraud losses probably still amount to a disturbingly high number.

And here is an additional perspective: The price of implementing the most effective anti-fraud controls—including financial controls, operational controls, physical security of inventory, employee training, hotlines, detailed fraud assessments, audits, and the like—would never amount to more than one-tenth the amount of money lost to fraud in a given year.

Remember

It is highly risky to assume that your organization is adequately protected against fraud. Even with the best controls in place, clever criminals will always find ways around them.

▶ The Urgency of Detecting and Preventing Fraud

With your understanding about the enormity of the fraud threat, together with the above clarification of the definition of fraud, you now have a foundation for moving ahead into the nitty gritty of major types of fraud, as well as the motives of those who commit them and the proven techniques for detecting and reporting incidents of fraud.

As you can see from Exhibit 1.3, internal audits and controls play a key role in the detection of fraud. Unfortunately, because of their general lack of training in fraud detection, the role of internal auditors and other financial professionals in fraud detection is *not* as significant as it should be: detection by accident and by employee or outsider tip rank higher. That is one important reason why learning to detect and report fraud is among the overarching purposes of this workbook.

There is some good news. Many frauds *can* be prevented! There are *many* ways to detect and report fraud before it does serious damage to your organization's reputation and financial health.

To make significant progress in fraud reduction, internal financial staff *must* play a decisive role in fraud detection. This workbook will provide solid guidance in how to use audit and other detection methods to discover fraudulent activity in your organization and when and how to report it so that senior management can determine whether to launch investigations of incidents of fraud or take other measures to rid the organization of fraud.

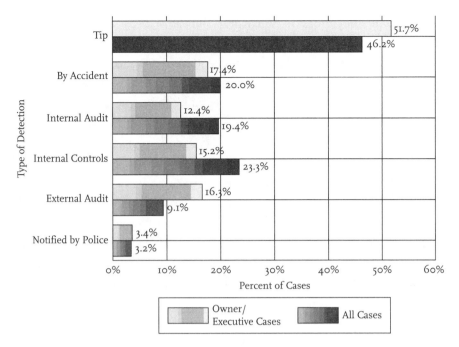

Exhibit 1.3 Initial Detection of Frauds by Owners/Executives

The sum of percentages exceeds 100 percent because in some cases respondents identified more than one detection method.

Source: ACFE *2008 Report to the Nation on Occupational Fraud and Abuse.*

Remember

Employees play a crucial role in detecting incidents of misconduct. Experience shows that under the right circumstances, employees *will* report fraud before it gets out of hand. Equally important in reducing fraud risk are properly executed internal fraud audits and anti-fraud processes and procedures—all aimed at detecting fraud before it does significant financial or reputational damage.

▶ Tone at the Top

You may have heard the term *tone at the top* in discussions about fraud or ethics. What does it mean, and why should you be concerned about it?

Tone at the top is best described as leading by good example. When top management of any organization lives by the standards of integrity and ethics that are set out in its Code of Conduct and, ideally an accompanying Anti-Fraud Policy, employees throughout the organization get the message that activities such as harassing co-workers, discriminating against minorities, engaging in conflicts of interest, and all types of fraud are strictly forbidden.

Another commonly used term for this is "Zero Tolerance" toward fraud. As long as management demonstrates its commitment to zero tolerance—without exception—there is a very good chance that employees throughout the ranks will conduct themselves in a similar way.

By contrast, consider the situation where the top bosses *say* they believe in ethics, but routinely award lucrative contracts to businesses in which they have a conflicting financial interest or falsify financial documents to persuade bankers to lend the organization money or accept kickbacks from vendors who are not well-equipped to deliver the goods or services needed by the organization.

Put another way, a company with good tone at the top is one whose top executive team and board of directors walk the talk with regard to integrity, honesty, and commitment to zero tolerance of unethical or criminal conduct. In this type of company, the doors of the management team are always open to employees at all levels to report or ask questions about fraud and ethical issues. In these companies, management's commitment to employees is openly demonstrated by taking modest bonuses and rewarding excellence and creative thinking throughout the employee population. Management's insistence on unconditional adherence to high standards of ethical conduct is exemplified by swift and decisive investigative and disciplinary action whenever instances of fraud do become known.

By contrast, Enron was an extreme example of an organization with negative tone at the top. There, executives set the example of abject disregard for responsible corporate leadership, greed, contempt for ethics, and habitual violation of major regulatory and legal standards. Unfortunately, similar behavior is still hitting the headlines almost every day.

Remember

Management and the board must walk the talk regarding the organization's values and integrity. *Lip service is deadly.*

▶ Review Points

- **History of fraud.** Fraud has been around from the beginning of time. But the world has gotten better at catching the bad guys over the centuries. Nonetheless, the problem persists, making it necessary for you to inform yourself about the current forms of fraud and how to prevent them.

- **Definitions of fraud.** There are several, but some are more accurate than others.

- **Statistical picture of fraud.** The numbers do not lie: Fraud is a *huge* worldwide problem—for all organizations.

- **Myths about fraud.** It is easy to become complacent about fraud, but this can be very costly.

- **Main types of fraud.** There are more ways than anyone could imagine by which fraudsters ply their trade.

- **How fraud is detected.** The main way is by tips from employees and outsiders. But internal auditors and financial managers can enhance their ability to detect fraud.

► **Chapter Quiz**

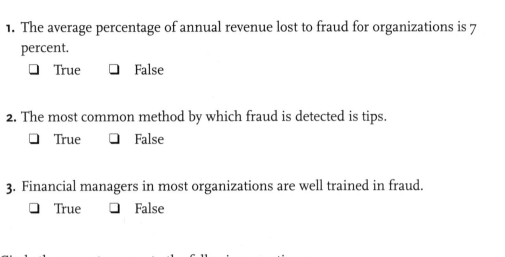

True or False:

1. The average percentage of annual revenue lost to fraud for organizations is 7 percent.
   ❏ True   ❏ False

2. The most common method by which fraud is detected is tips.
   ❏ True   ❏ False

3. Financial managers in most organizations are well trained in fraud.
   ❏ True   ❏ False

Circle the correct answer to the following questions:

4. The average amount of money lost to fraudulent financial reporting fraud is
   a. $100,000
   b. $1 million
   c. $ 2 million
   d. $ 5 million

5. The new U.S. law enacted to prevent financial statement fraud is the
   a. Securities Act of 1933
   b. COSO Act of 1985
   c. Sarbanes Oxley Act of 2002
   d. Securities and Exchange Commission Act

6. Cooking the books is a form of
   a. Stealing
   b. Deception
   c. Concealment
   d. Misleading

7. Circle the choice below that is *not* one of the myths about fraud:
   a. Ethics and Compliance training has us covered.
   b. Our finance staff are qualified to protect the organization against fraud.
   c. Fraud is an unavoidable cost of doing business.
   d. Fraud is a problem for law enforcement.

Fill in the blank:

8. *Leading by example* is a term similar in meaning to _____.

9. The main objective of this workbook is to help you learn how to prevent, detect, and _____ fraud.

10. The place for spelling out the organization's concept of leading by example for employees to see is in its _____.

For the answers, please turn to Appendix A.

CHAPTER TWO

The Human Element of Fraud

As discussed in Chapter 1, there is ample statistical evidence that fraud poses a serious threat—not only to your organization, but to *all* organizations and the employees who work for them. Many fraud prevention experts use the so-called 20-60-20 rule to illustrate the human component of fraud:

- Approximately 20 percent of the people in any organization will never steal—no matter what. They are people whose character and integrity are so strong that nothing could pressure or tempt them to do anything dishonest.

- Another 60 percent of the people in the organization are fence sitters. They are basically honest people. But if given the *opportunity* to commit fraud and the risk seems minimal to them, they might cross the line.

- The remaining 20 percent are fundamentally dishonest. They will always commit fraud when the opportunity arises. In fact they will often try to create opportunities to steal or deceive if they think they will gain financially.

Statistics give perspective on the vastness of the fraud problem, but they do not teach us what we really need to know in order to *combat* fraud, namely:

- Who commits fraud
- Who the victims are
- Who prevents fraud

Fraud does not occur by itself; it is a *human* invention. The many varieties of fraud are all creations of men and women. Similarly, people are the ultimate victims of fraud—even in cases where a huge corporation, not-for-profit, or government agency is the *apparent* victim. This chapter shows that in these frauds, more than the bottom line is damaged. Human lives also suffer when an employer gets hit by fraud.

We are all on the frontline against frauds of all types. This chapter demonstrates that only *people* have the power to prevent, detect, and report fraud.

Note. According to several experts, the portion of total fraud committed by insiders ranges from over 50% to as much as 80%. Chapter 3 focuses on external fraud; however, much of what follows in this chapter applies primarily to *internal* fraud.

To keep the vast topic of internal fraud as simple as possible, it is helpful to divide it into two key categories (Exhibit 2.1):

- **Employee-level fraud.** This type of fraud is committed by people who are neither supervisors nor managers or executives. They may be salaried professionals or hourly employees.

- **Management-level fraud.** These crimes are committed by managers at all levels—including the most senior levels. Many of the frauds committed by these individuals are the same as those committed by employees lower down the organization chart.

Key distinction. Though committed with less frequency than frauds committed at the employee level, virtually *all* management level frauds result in much greater losses than those perpetrated at lower levels.

The reason is clear. Managers have more authority and therefore more opportunity to cheat than those who work under them.

Important. For the same reason, proportionately greater financial losses also result from frauds that only managers and executives have the authority to commit. Later chapters discuss such potentially costly management frauds as financial reporting fraud, concealing material financial facts, and high-level bribery.

Example. A typical management-level fraud is the kind that involves fraudulent financial reporting, such as in the Enron case, which ultimately resulted in the total collapse of the company. By contrast, typical employee-level frauds include padding expense reimbursement claims or diverting checks that are payable to vendors.

■ The Fraud Personality: Soft Indicators

As you will learn shortly, there is useful theoretical analysis about the motives for employees to commit fraud. But there are also key behavioral indicators common to most internal fraudsters. By recognizing them, we can often prevent fraud or at least intervene before it causes excessive damage. We call these "soft indicators" of fraud, since they are intangible and lack hard evidence. They are, however, potentially very valuable in detecting potential fraud.

Remember

There is an inverse ratio between the level of the organization at which fraud is committed and the amount of financial loss resulting from frauds at each level. Thus, while management-level frauds are committed less frequently than employee-level frauds, the financial loss resulting from these crimes is almost always significantly greater than the amount lost to frauds committed by lower-level employees.

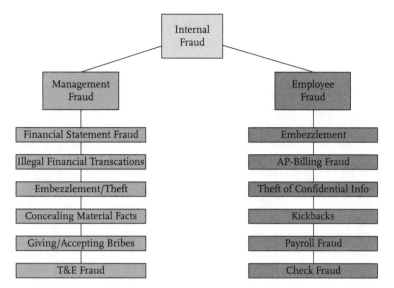

Internal Fraud

Management Fraud
- Financial Statement Fraud
- Illegal Financial Transcations
- Embezzlement/Theft
- Concealing Material Facts
- Giving/Accepting Bribes
- T&E Fraud

Employee Fraud
- Embezzlement
- AP-Billing Fraud
- Theft of Confidential Info
- Kickbacks
- Payroll Fraud
- Check Fraud

Exhibit 2.1   The Two Levels of Internal Fraud

Common soft indicators include:

- **Weak sense of ethics.** A co-worker whose behavior clearly indicates a lack of respect for the basic standard of doing the right thing—by constantly lying, deceiving, or maliciously undermining others for no apparent reason—may be equally willing to commit fraud.

- **Risk-taking.** People who act in ways that could get them into trouble by, for example, driving excessively fast, gambling, living beyond their means, and so on may also find it easy to steal from their employer.

  Important. This behavior is similar to a dislike for working inside the system. People who think the rules do not apply to them or who enjoy beating the system may also be prone to exploiting opportunities to steal or commit other types of fraud.

- **Refusal to take time off.** People who are committing fraud at work are likely to fear being caught if they go on vacation. Doing so gives others the opportunity to snoop around the employee's work space, creating the risk of discovering evidence of fraud.

- **Coming in early or staying late.** This can be a sign that someone is trying to hide incriminating evidence or needs privacy to commit fraud.

- **Abuse of drugs or alcohol.** These are expensive habits that create financial pressures that could lead an employee to think about stealing.

- **Sudden or unusual mood swings.** Normally cheerful, relaxed people who suddenly show signs of impatience, tension, or irritability may be suffering from guilt related to illegal conduct that they have or are about to engage in. Or they may be dealing poorly with mounting financial pressures that may eventually drive them to commit fraud.

- **Showing up at work with possessions beyond their financial means.** A person who starts driving to work in an expensive luxury car may have inherited money from a relative. But more often than not, he is stealing to support an excessive lifestyle.

■ The Fraud Personality: Hard Indicators

In contrast, hard indicators are pieces of evidence that are *tangible*. They are *not* personality traits, but rather signs of fraud represented by numerical oddities or by physical evidence. For example:

- Forged or altered checks
- Evidence of new, unfamiliar vendors showing up in accounts payable
- Sudden jumps in prices paid for frequently-purchased materials
- Invoices lacking key information such as the vendor's full address or invoice number
- Losses of physical assets/supplies from warehouses
- Unusual increases in payroll amounts or duplicate paychecks going to a single employee
- Altered or totally fabricated invoices
- Computer evidence of manipulating sensitive financial data
- Missing blank checks
- Ghost employees on the payroll records (Non-existent employees with addresses matching those of employees with access to the organization's payroll records and computer systems)
- Evidence of padding expenses, such as phony receipts, absence of receipts, charges for items or services that are clearly of a personal nature

▶ Why People Steal

There are innumerable varieties of fraud that must be screened for and prevented whenever possible. However, merely understanding the mechanics of these frauds is not enough to minimize the risk that your organization will be victimized by the bad guys. You must first understand the motives and mindset of fraudsters.

This is often difficult to do when talking about external fraudsters. These are people whom we usually do not know and may never know. However, most external fraudsters' motives for committing fraud are primarily related to character—many outside fraudsters simply lack the ethical values that keep honest people on the right side of the law. This means that many external fraudsters are career criminals, with long histories of illegal activity.

Other external fraudsters are in it for the thrill. These are people who do not make a living committing fraud, but who love the excitement of risk taking and enjoy pushing the envelope to prove how good they are at getting away with criminal acts.

For example, the stereotypical youthful computer whiz who holes up in his parents' basement with a console of computer monitors and spends hours figuring out how to hack into the secure databases of major retail chains to steal consumer credit card data. He is typically motivated more by the excitement and pursuit of bragging rights among his peers than he is by the prospect of making a lot of money by selling the stolen data.

By contrast, when it comes to *internal* fraudsters, the story is much different. We are often familiar with the personalities, character traits, and behavioral patterns of these people. This means with the proper knowledge about what drives insiders to commit fraud, we can often detect the tell-tale behavioral and circumstantial indicators that someone may be about to break the law, which makes it possible to stop a fraud before it occurs or at least before it can do serious financial damage.

■ The Fraud Triangle

One set of factors common to internal fraudsters *at all levels in the organization* is the Fraud Triangle. The theory behind the Fraud Triangle was developed in the 1940s by a leading criminologist, Donald Cressey, who conducted extensive research with convicted embezzlers to determine what motivated seemingly honest people to commit fraud.

His research led him to coin the term, "trust violators" to describe people who embezzle. According to Cressey's research, "Trusted persons become trust violators when they conceive of themselves as having a financial problem which is 'nonsharable,' are aware this problem can be secretly resolved by violation of the position of financial trust, and are able to apply to their own conduct in that situation verbalizations which enable them to adjust their conceptions of themselves as trusted persons with their conceptions of themselves as users of the entrusted fund or property."[1]

This somewhat convoluted language essentially means that people who are experiencing severe financial problems about which they are embarrassed (or for other reasons cannot discuss with others) find ways to commit fraud—thinking that they will not get caught while convincing themselves that they are doing nothing wrong.

Eventually, Cressey's findings came to be summed up in what is now widely referred to as the Fraud Triangle. The three components of the Fraud Triangle are—just as Cressey suggests in more complex wording—Pressure, Opportunity, and Rationalization. See Exhibit 2.2.

Pressure in the context of the Fraud Triangle typically is the direct result of excessive credit card debt, mountains of unpaid health care bills, out-of-control gambling debts, extended unemployment, or similar financial difficulties.

Opportunity exists when an employee discovers a weakness in the organization's anti-fraud controls. Such a weakness might exist, for example, if an employee authorized to issue purchase orders (POs) also reviews and approves delivery documentation. That employee could have all or part of deliveries diverted to a location of her own choosing or to a fence who pays for the goods in cash. The fraudster then falsifies the delivery documents to make it appear as though her company received the order according the specifications of the PO. This may also require doctoring inventory records to avoid discrepancies between delivery and inventory records. This can often be done by altering the copy of the delivery documents that goes to inventory to make it appear that the order was rejected or was short.

Exhibit 2.2 The Fraud Triangle

Rationalization—the third element of the Fraud Triangle—is a psychological process in which a person who has committed fraud convinces himself that the act is either not wrong or that, even though it may be wrong, it will be corrected because he will eventually return the money. Another, often more damaging form of rationalization occurs when the employee justifies the fraud by taking the attitude that she *deserves* the stolen money—because the company was unfair by denying her a raise or promotion or that some other form of mistreatment made the individual a "victim."

Cressey's theory teaches that when all three of these elements are in place in an individual's life, he is very likely to commit fraud (or already has).

◀ **Case Study #1**

Pain, Pills, and Petty Cash

Deena, a bookkeeper for Jones Printing Company (not an actual company) is on an annual salary of $30,000 and has a husband and three children. One day, while running some errands, she suffered a serious fall and broke her left leg and several ribs. She was in intense pain for many weeks while she was healing. During that period her doctor prescribed powerful pain killers, which he cautioned her to use only as prescribed because they can be very addictive.

But Deena's pain was so intense and relentless that she gradually took more and more of the pain-killing pills. After two months the pain had subsided, but she found she did not feel normal unless she continued to take the pills. When she ran out of them, she asked her doctor for more. He refused, indicating that she no longer needed the pills and again warned her that they are highly addictive.

So she began ordering the pills from Internet suppliers at a cost of $200 per month. After several months, she had gone through a good portion of the family's modest savings and was worried about how she would continue to finance her addiction. Fearing her husband's wrath, she kept the whole problem a secret.

Thanks to her position as a bookkeeper at Jones Printing, Deena had access to the business's checks. This presented an enormous temptation to her as she imagined different ways that she could issue checks to herself, deposit them in her bank account and use the cash to continue buying the pain killers on the Internet.

However, as an honest person who had never broken the law before, Deena struggled with the decision of whether to commit this fraud. Eventually, after reasoning that the chances of getting caught were low, and promising herself that she would pay the money back when she stopped taking the drugs, she decided to go ahead and write a check on one of Jones Printing's accounts to cash for $200. She charged the payment to Petty Cash, forged her manager's signature, deposited the check in her personal bank account, and purchased a fresh supply of pain killers. After two weeks, when she was running low again on the drug, she wrote another check for $200.

This pattern continued until she was no longer able to make it through the day even on a large dosage of the drug. Eventually, she began arriving at work late and performing substandard work.

Her colleagues began to suspect something was wrong with her. An audit of the books revealed that monthly totals for Petty Cash were five times what they normally were. Deena's fraud was discovered, and she was terminated.

The Fraud Triangle Lesson:

- Deena's nonsharable financial Pressure came when she had dipped into the family savings and became desperate for cash to pay for her drugs. She could not share her problem with anyone for fear of disapproval, rejection, and other unpleasant consequences.

- The Opportunity presented itself by virtue of her job. As a bookkeeper, she had a perfect opportunity to embezzle money from her employer to pay for her drugs.

- Finally, the Rationalization came as Deena convinced herself that she was not stealing the money—she was only borrowing it and would pay it back when she kicked her habit.

How could this fraud have been prevented? List as many controls as you can. Compare yours with those listed in Appendix B.

1. _____

2. _____

3. _____

■ Other Fraud Triangle Factors

Deena's pressures, opportunities and rationalizations in Case Study # 1 are just one illustration of many types of each element of the Fraud Triangle to beware of in your daily activities. Following are several additional ones to watch for:

Common Pressures	Common Opportunities	Common Rationalizations
High medical expenses	Access to blank checks	"I'm only borrowing the money."
Sudden life crises—divorce, death	Access to financial records	"I deserve the extra money" for the family, and so on.
Gambling addiction	Access to cash	"My bosses are dishonest, so I can do what they're doing."

■ A Triangle or a Diamond?

In recent years a variation on the Fraud Triangle theory has emerged among anti-fraud professionals. It has been dubbed the "Fraud Diamond" due to the inclusion of a *fourth* psychological motive for employees to commit fraud.

This motive often manifests itself most significantly during economic downturns or recessions. That is because negative economic cycles result in mass layoffs, pay cuts, loss of benefits, and other unfavorable effects. This in turn causes employees who still have jobs to become nervous about their positions in the organization while at the same time resenting management for having fired their friends and co-workers. These employees lose their sense of loyalty or dedication to their employers, and this disenfranchisement in many instances plays itself out in the form of fraudulent conduct, and people may think to themselves, *Management doesn't care about its people* or *We employees are obviously not that important to the organization, so I'm going to take what I can get as long as I can.*

The critical lesson here is that it is top management's job to *prevent* the culture of a Fraud Diamond from taking root in the organization. Essential to achieving this goal is appropriate tone at the top (see Chapter 1).

Still, this is never easy, especially when seemingly more important pressures—such as sustaining revenues and profits—are weighing excessively on the organization's top decision makers. However, downplaying the importance of this management duty can result in costly fraud.

Remember

The theory behind the Fraud Triangle reveals much about which employees are likely to commit fraud, why they do it, and how they convince themselves that they are not doing anything wrong. This in turn shows that people we might never expect to commit a fraud are leading personal lives that comprise the elements of the Fraud Triangle.

▪ The Trust Factor

An equally important psychological factor that often causes organizations to become victims of fraud is the Trust Factor. This is a natural and usually overlooked tendency on the part of an organization's managers to automatically trust those who work for them. It is rooted in the basic human inclination to assume that people who work for you are honest, loyal, dedicated, and would never *think* of committing fraud.

Unfortunately, in more cases than you would want to know about, employees exploit this trust to commit fraud against their employers, knowing that they will not be suspected of wrongdoing. Amazingly, many of these are rookie criminals. They never stole a dime from anyone until they stole from the company. This was especially surprising when it occurred in a nonprofit organization devoted to helping people kick their substance abuse habits:

◄ Case Study #2

The Trusted Thief

Scott Caldwell entered Harvest House Ministries, a Canadian drug and alcohol rehabilitation facility, to try to kick a severe case of alcoholism. He got sober, and while he was residing at Harvest House he worked hard on—and ultimately earned—a professional accounting certificate. By this time, Scott was well-known to everyone at Harvest House, and thanks to his pleasant personality, had become well-liked—even trusted.

So trusted was Scott by the directors of the organization, that they offered him a full-time job as a bookkeeper. He was given full authority to handle Harvest House's day-to-day financial transactions and maintain its financial records. To Scott, nothing more wonderful could have happened. Everything went along fine for about five years and Scott proved to be a reliable employee. Until . . .

A long-overdue surprise audit revealed that Scott had been diverting Harvest House funds to his own personal accounts for three full years. He had managed to embezzle about $300,000 from the charity's payroll and fundraising accounts before the audit revealed his fraud.[*]

Lesson for all. People you trust and least expect to commit fraud are all too often exactly the ones you need to be careful about.

How could this fraud have been prevented? List as many controls as you can. Compare yours with those listed in Appendix B.

1. _____

2. _____

3. _____

[*]Source: www2.canada.com/ottawacitizen/news/city/story.html?id=c06ecea3-8b15-4e8b-a770-288b18fceab6.

This and other scenarios like it should *not* lead you to think that you cannot trust *anyone* you work with. But it does illustrate the importance of maintaining a degree of skepticism in your day-to-day work activities.

The same holds true in your personal life. Just think about how many new stories you've heard about a trusted, seemingly respectable investment advisor or broker making off with millions—or even *billions*—of his clients' money. These clients put their unqualified trust in their investment advisors, without first doing background research on them in public records such as news archives, government databases, court filings, and Internet postings to learn if there was anything shady or sinister that would make them think twice before handing over their hard-earned dollars.

The $50 billion Ponzi scheme perpetrated by famed Wall Street investment advisor Bernard Madoff is one of the most stunning cases of such abuse of trust, and of the absence of skepticism on the part of institutions that should have been monitoring his activities.

▶ People: The Key to Detection and Prevention

It is true, as you will learn shortly, that anti-fraud professionals, auditors, financial managers, and senior managers now have highly effective technology tools to detect and investigate fraud. However, anti-fraud software and electronic information resources are only as good as the individuals using them.

More important, even the most wonderful high-tech anti-fraud tools are not foolproof. We must still rely on people to detect indicators of possible fraudulent activity and to blow the whistle.

Anti-fraud professionals generally agree that having the knowledge to *Prevent*, *Detect* and *Report* fraud is not enough to cut fraud losses. They therefore advise management to make it the *responsibility* of everyone in the organization to use that knowledge to *take action* against fraud. We call this the P-D-R Responsibility. It means that you, the financial professional, have a duty to recognize the red flags of the major types of fraud so you can take action by reporting incidents to your superior, by using the organization's confidential hotline, or by using any other reporting channel that may be available to you. If you are unfamiliar with or unsure about how to use these reporting mechanisms, or if you have questions about what is expected of you with regard to detecting and reporting fraud, consult your supervisor, a senior Human Resources manager, or a compliance official.

Important. When we talk about P-D-R Responsibility, we do not just mean protecting your organization against fraud. We also mean protecting the employees for whom it provides jobs and the customers who benefit from its services, because when fraud hits an organization, it hurts everyone who works there, including you.

Here again, the Enron case provides a helpful example. In that historic fraud, perpetrated by the company's top executives by creating fictitious financial reports to disguise the company's massive losses, the end result was bankruptcy. Far worse, though, thousands of innocent employees lost their jobs, their health benefits, and even their pensions.

Enron is an extreme example of how fraud that hurts an organization hurts its employees. But other incidents of fraud can also harm employees. For example, if enough money is lost to fraudsters, the organization may be forced to:

- Reduce or eliminate pay increases
- Cut back on health and pension benefits
- Lay off workers
- Freeze career advancement opportunities

The bottom line. If your organization's policies make it your duty to prevent, detect, and report fraud, remember that doing so is also in your personal interest. And even if they do not, you *still* have the same personal interest in doing what you can to take action against fraud.

◀ Case Study #3

Demise by Personal Debt

A food distribution company with 150 employees was experiencing financial problems. The board engaged a local auditor to review the books. The auditor discovered that the company's two co-founders had accumulated over $150,000 in credit card debt on their business credit cards.

Further investigation determined that the majority of the credit card charges were for personal expenses rather than business-related ones. Before a solution could be implemented, the company was forced to file for bankruptcy. All except a skeletal staff of employees immediately lost their jobs.

How could this fraud have been prevented? List as many controls as you can. Compare yours with those listed in Appendix B.

1. _____

2. _____

3. _____

▶ Review Points

- Only *people* are able to detect and prevent fraud.
- Approximately 80 percent of all employees are fundamentally honest, but the opportunities to commit fraud are often so tempting to many employees that they decide to cross the line.

- The Fraud Triangle (Pressure, Opportunity, and Rationalization) helps to explain the motives of employees to steal from their employers.
- A fourth motivator—disenfranchisement—can transform the Fraud Triangle into a Fraud Diamond.
- Tone at the top is the example set by top executives and the board regarding the organization's commitment to ethical standards. To influence employees to conduct themselves in an honest and trustworthy manner, management must walk the talk regarding its attitude and policies on fraud.
- The Trust Factor inadvertently creates opportunities for employees to commit fraud. This is the natural tendency for bosses and co-workers to trust each other to be honest, giving dishonest people opportunities to commit fraud without raising suspicion. It teaches us that doing our day-to-day work with an element of professional skepticism can be very helpful in detecting fraudulent or suspicious conduct.
- It is in *everyone's* interest to Prevent, Detect, and Report fraud. The P-D-R Responsibility that everyone has for fighting fraud—Prevent-Detect-Report—is emphasized throughout this workbook.
- The four personal harmful effects fraud can cause when an organization is victimized by internal fraud are:
    - Reduced or eliminated pay increases
    - Cutbacks on health and pension benefits
    - Laid off workers
    - Frozen career advancement opportunities
- In addition to the Fraud Triangle, there are distinct soft and hard indicators that fraud is being perpetrated by your employees.

► Chapter Quiz

True or False:

1. Tone at the top is effective when management sets an example of the company's commitment to integrity.
    ❑ True   ❑ False

2. Mass layoffs can result in emergence of a fourth motive for fraud, transforming the Fraud Triangle into a Fraud Diamond.
    ❑ True   ❑ False

Circle the correct answer to the following questions:

3. In the 20-60-20 rule, all except one of the following choices are correct. Pick the choice that is *incorrect*:
    a. 20 percent of employees will *never* steal.

b. 60 percent of employees are fundamentally honest but *could* be tempted to cross the line.

c. 20 percent of employees will commit fraud *only* if other employees do.

4. The percentage of fraud committed by insiders—people who work for an organization—is as much as:

   a. 20 percent

   b. 56 percent

   c. 80 percent

5. The Fraud Triangle includes:

   a. Opportunity, Rationalization, and Disenfranchisement

   b. Pressure, Opportunity, and Trust

   c. Pressure, Integrity, and Rationalization

   d. Pressure, Opportunity, and Rationalization

6. When fraud is committed, it may result in all except one of the following. Pick the choice that does *not* apply:

   a. Layoffs

   b. Elimination of health benefits and/or pensions

   c. Reduced employment opportunities at other organizations

Fill in the blank:

7. The P-D-R Responsibility obligates you to Prevent, Detect, and _____ fraud.

8. When we refer to taking action against fraud, we mean calling the organization's confidential hotline or informing your _____.

9. Showing up for work at odd hours and refusing to take vacation are _____ indicators of possible fraud.

For the answers, please turn to Appendix A.

CHAPTER THREE

Internal Fraud: Employee Level

Avoid jumping into this chapter with preconceptions about the typical internal fraudster. While there are some general characteristics common to most insiders who commit fraud, you may one day be totally surprised when someone you completely trusted, someone who would never do anything wrong, someone whom you looked up to, or even someone at the very top of the executive ladder, gets arrested for committing fraud.

Important. This is not to suggest that you should not trust anyone you work with. In fact, most of your co-workers are basically honest. But sometimes people get into jams, and they feel they have no way out other than to steal from their employer.

As you will learn in the coming pages, there are thousands of ways to do this and almost as many ways to rationalize such criminal behavior. In keeping with the purpose of this workbook—to provide you with the knowledge and know-how to Prevent, Detect and Report fraud—you will learn about the intricacies of internal fraud for the purpose of helping your organization reduce its exposure to fraudsters—*not* for the purpose of undermining the workplace environment by suspecting that everyone is a potential criminal.

▶ How Big a Problem Is Internal Fraud?

Estimates vary, but nearly all research on internal fraud concludes that crimes by insiders against their employers represent a far greater threat than external fraud. Though such external frauds as vendor schemes, social engineering, and pretexting can result in enormous losses and reputational damage, the $994 *billion* lost to fraud each year, as mentioned in Chapter 1, represents the ACFE's estimate of the total *internal* fraud losses. And, as discussed in Chapter 2, according to numerous experts, internal fraud represents the majority of all fraud affecting an average organization.

This is why the topics covered in this chapter are the 800-pound gorilla with regard to fraud. The chapter demonstrates not only how devastating the financial damage of internal fraud can be, but also how insiders who commit the vast array of such frauds can be very creative in their dishonest activities.

Remember

Chapter Two showed that fraud is a human issue. This chapter reveals some fascinating—and even surprising—findings about what makes people cross the line, how they do it, and who suffers the consequences. The chapter also discusses how to prevent insider fraud, which is, again, among the major themes of this Workbook.

▶ Overview of Employee-Level Fraud

Internal fraud occurs at two main levels: the employee level and the management level. The rest of this chapter will focuses on employee-level fraud, with management-level fraud covered in Chapter 4.

Major Types of Internal Employee-Level Fraud Discussed in This Chapter

- Embezzlement
- Accounts payable (AP) fraud
- Kickback schemes
- Inventory/supply schemes
- Check fraud and tampering
- Travel and entertainment (T&E) fraud
- Payroll schemes
- Theft of confidential information
- Insider abuse of computer systems

The following pages examine each of these types of internal employee-level fraud —some of which overlap with each other—and demonstrate how to recognize the red flags and how to report incidents of these crimes or suspicious indicators that they may be occurring.

■ Embezzlement

Embezzlement is—by far—the most common form of employee-level fraud. There are literally countless ways by which embezzlement can be committed. But the main ones to be concerned about are:

- Accounts payable (AP) and billing fraud
- Accounts receivable fraud (including lapping, skimming, and theft of cash)
- Kickback schemes
- Inventory/supply theft
- Check fraud and tampering
- Travel and entertainment (T&E) fraud
- Payroll schemes

■ Accounts Payable (AP) Fraud

Accounts payable (AP) or billing fraud occurs when employees abuse their access or control over the disbursements/payables processes to steal funds, or when employees without such authority exploit weaknesses in the organization's AP fraud-prevention measures. Billing schemes perpetrated by insiders undoubtedly represent one of the most common and costly forms of fraud. As such, numerous varieties of billing fraud must be watched for by AP staff, anti-fraud personnel, and senior management.

Some of the many ways that AP-related embezzlement is committed include:

- Billing schemes
  - Shell company frauds
  - Submitting phony invoices
  - Unauthorized purchases
  - Collusion/corruption
- Theft of confidential information
- Inventory theft
- Vendor Master File fraud
- Check fraud/tampering and Automated Clearing House (ACH) fraud
- Collusion (with co-workers and/or with vendors)
- Purchasing card (P-Card) fraud

Setting up phony vendors and generating false invoices to be paid by the organization is among the most common and varied categories of billing fraud. These are not companies at all, but rather businesses in name only. They are created by employees with the intention of generating bogus invoices in the "company's" name and submitting them to their employer for payment. These perpetrators are often procurement or accounts payable staffers or higher-ups who have the authority to approve payments.

The perpetrators usually set up a bank account in the entity's name, using fraudulent incorporation documents that they obtain for as little as $80 depending on which state they are located in. (If they are too cheap to spring for the fee and too lazy to fill out the incorporation documents, they may simply create counterfeit incorporation documents and use those to open a business bank account.) After that, it is a simple matter of cranking out bogus invoices in the "vendor's" name using a basic PC and an inexpensive printer.

But what if an employee is not in a position with the authority to approve phony invoices and get them routed through the payments process? Sometimes, criminals will get around this by entering into a collusive scheme with a co-worker who *does* have the requisite authority.

Others generate phony purchase orders (POs) for goods or services that the company purchases on a regular basis and forge an authorized manager's signature. They then generate the phony invoices for the shell company and await payment.

Another common form of phony vendor fraud involves creating a shell company with a name very similar to a legitimate vendor that the organization regularly makes payments to—but with a different address. For example, a phony vendor with the name of J.R. Maintenance Company may be completely phony but its bogus invoices may get paid and credited to the organization's legitimate vendor, J.R. Maintenance Inc., despite the latter's different address.

Another common form of billing scheme involves employees making unauthorized purchases. When employees have the authority to initiate or approve purchases

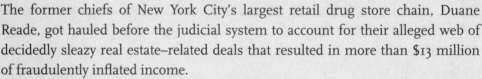

◄ Case Study #4

Shell Game in the Big Apple

The former chiefs of New York City's largest retail drug store chain, Duane Reade, got hauled before the judicial system to account for their alleged web of decidedly sleazy real estate–related deals that resulted in more than $13 million of fraudulently inflated income.

In New York City, where Duane Reade had more than 200 retail stores in the late 1990s, it was not uncommon for landlords to offer early termination buyouts of existing retail store leases in order to rent the space to new tenants at higher rates. Duane Reade accepted several of these legitimate so-called real estate concession deals. But then Anthony Cuti, Duane Reade's former CEO and William Tennant, the company's former Real Estate Administrator and CFO, got greedy. As a result of their shenanigans, they were charged by the SEC with numerous frauds involving phony transfers of retail leases to shell company landlords in exchange for payments used to doctor the company's books before being repaid to the shell company "principals."

In most of their "deals," Cuti and Tennant relied on a single real estate broker to negotiate its leases. Working with Tennant, the broker ultimately came to serve as Duane Reade's real estate department—conducting most of the company's real estate–related administrative functions, including maintaining and updating a list of Duane Reade's real estate holdings, and its rights and obligations with respect to those holdings, and negotiating with landlords in over 90 percent of the company's real estate transactions.

When Cuti first approached the principals and told them that he wanted them to pay Duane Reade for an option to purchase certain real estate rights, the principals objected and told Cuti that the option had no value. Cuti replied that if they (the principals) did not do the deal and pay Duane Reade, he would find another brokerage firm that would. Cuti committed to repay the principals through separate transactions, and promised that they would break even on the real estate concession transactions. Based on these promises, and because Duane Reade represented the majority of the broker's business, the principals agreed to participate in the Cuti deals.

How it worked. At Cuti's suggestion, the principals set up two shell companies—"Shell A" and "Shell B"—to act as counterparties on Duane Reade's real estate concession contracts. For about three-and-a-half years, Cuti structured and Tennant implemented at least 13 sham real estate concession transactions between Duane Reade and the principals through their shell companies.

The transactions were typically concluded at the end of a quarter, or after the end of the quarter and backdated. Despite their lack of any financial value, Cuti and Tennant structured the transactions so that the payments would appear to be legitimate concession payments, and Cuti and Tennant convinced Duane Reade management and its auditors that the payments should therefore be recognized as current income.

Key. To complete the fraud, and to minimize the impact of the repayments on current income, they disguised the repayments—paid to the principals through the shell companies or the broker—as "compensation for brokerage services" or for amounts that were deliberately inflated.

How could this fraud have been prevented? List as many controls as you can. Compare yours with those listed in Appendix B.

1. _____

2. _____

3. _____

and decide to exploit this authority to criminal ends, they may initiate orders for goods that they, rather than their employer, actually receive.

Such schemes are often easy to pull off if the offender is a professional in a special area such as computers or telecommunications and the manager approving purchase requests is not sufficiently familiar with the nature of the goods or services being ordered—or is the perpetrator *herself*.

Billing fraud can also be perpetrated through the use of what are referred to as "straw vendor" schemes. Also known as "pass-through vendor" schemes, these crimes occur when an employee who is in a position to approve invoices and authorize payments sets up a bogus company and has that company order goods that his or her employer actually needs—from a legitimate vendor. The goods in turn are sold to the organization at inflated prices. The invoices are approved by the fraudster. The fraudster may even be able to generate bogus refunds or rebates to the straw vendor, which he controls.[1]

If your organization uses procurement cards (P-cards), commonly referred to as corporate credit cards, you may be pleased to learn that only 13 percent of organizations were victims of business-to-business P-Card fraud in 2007, according to the Association for Financial Professionals (AFP).[2]

Nonetheless, the remaining 87 percent of organizations are not necessarily immune to P-Card fraud, which is why it is helpful for all AP personnel to know how P-Card fraud is committed and how to prevent it.

The key reason that organizations initiate P-card programs is to save money on the cost of processing business-related orders. Because it costs as much to process a $250 order as it does a $250,000 order using the organization's normal procurement system, consolidating numerous small orders through the use of P-cards can save more than 50 percent in processing costs, according to the National Association of Purchasing Card Professionals (NAPCP).

If you currently have responsibility for managing your organization's P-Card program, you probably have found that the majority of P-Card-related frauds are committed by noncardholders. According to the AFP, "Unknown external parties or employees [are] most likely to [be] the perpetrators of corporate card fraud."[3]

The important implication here is that P-Card data (such as card number, expiration date, and cardholder name) is being stolen by outsiders and used to make fraudulent purchases. These outsiders could be employees of merchant outlets from which one of your P-card holders made one or more purchases. Or they could be cyber thieves who hack into merchant databases and steal the card data of legitimate customers (such as your organization's P-card holders) and use the stolen information to perpetrate fraudulent transactions.

While nearly every state now requires companies to notify individuals whose information has been lost, regardless of whether it was accidentally disclosed or was stolen during a cyber attack, this is not always done promptly, and fraudulent use of the card may result in losses well before you become aware of the breach.[4]

Internally, of course, the problem arises when P-card users abuse their card privileges by making unauthorized or fraudulent purchases, thereby wiping out any cost efficiencies *and* causing fraud losses for their employers.

Fortunately, as discussed later in this chapter, there are effective anti-fraud controls to minimize your risk of being victimized by both internal and external P-Card fraudsters.

Finally on the list of leading billing schemes is what we will call "hybrid billing fraud." On the next page is a real-life example of how two brothers with a bright business future as health care company entrepreneurs lost everything by perpetrating a hybrid fraud combining billing/PO fraud, kickbacks, collusion, and shell company scams. Some frauds are not easily categorized into precise, neat definitions, but instead combine schemes from *multiple* categories.

In addition to the danger from billing fraud, your AP function is also a potential target for inventory theft and fraud, check fraud, and theft of confidential information.

Before moving on from AP fraud, though, it is important to address one additional form of such crime: Vendor Master File (VMF) fraud.

Any organization's VMF is a potentially ideal launch site for a whole arsenal of weapons of white-collar crime.

Naturally, many of these crimes ultimately fall into the category of vendor or billing fraud. But with access to the VMF, dishonest employees—or outsiders for that matter—have a much easier job of fabricating bogus vendors, generating fraudulent invoices, and obtaining approval of fraudulent transactions.

Health Care Fraud

As reported by the FBI, two brothers, Carlos and Jorge De Cespedes owned a Miami-based medical supply company called Pharmed and initiated a billing and corruption scheme that took advantage of Pharmed's vendor relationship with Kendall Regional Medical Center.

The scheme started modestly with Jorge De Cespedes, president and CEO of Pharmed, making a few cash payments to Sylvia Oramas, the director of material management for Kendall Regional, in exchange for medical supplies from Kendall Regional's medical supplies distribution center, HCA East Florida Consolidated Supply Center.

Building on the success of this scheme, De Cespedes and Oramas initiated a scheme that exploited key features of Kendall Regional's computerized supply management system known to users as SMART. To execute the scheme, Oramas recruited two co-conspirators—Joanna Delfel and Victor Garcia—both former Supply Center managers who had access to the SMART system. Delfel and Garcia used their own passwords, as well as passwords that they illegally acquired from other employees, to generate large-volume purchase orders for Pharmed supplies. They then falsely recorded delivery of the orders to Kendall Regional, thereby triggering payment by Kendall Regional to Pharmed for the bogus orders.

After receiving the fraudulent payments from Kendall Regional for the phantom orders, the De Cespedes brothers transferred the funds from Pharmed to various shell corporations they controlled. The funds were then further distributed from the De Cespedes brothers' shell corporations to Soho Marketing, Inc., another shell company controlled by Sylvia Oramas, and to Gator Sports Collectibles, Inc., yet another shell company, controlled by Erika Urquiza, the former Assistant Vice-President of Materials Management at Pharmed.

SoHo and Gator Sports in turn distributed the proceeds of the billing fraud to Oramas, Delfel, Garcia, and others.*

How could this fraud have been prevented? List as many controls as you can. Compare yours with those listed in Appendix B.

1. _____

2. _____

3. _____

*United States of America v. Carlos DeCespedes and Jorge DeCespedes, 08-20675-cr-Altonaga/Brown (S.D. Fla. 2008).

For example, an employee who has authorization to add new vendors to the VMF or make changes to existing ones can:

- Add completely bogus vendors and submit invoices as if the vendor were legitimate.
- Alter the mailing address of an inactive vendor
- Generate bogus invoices with her own or an accomplice's address

As your organization's business changes, so do the vendors it uses. However, too many organizations fail to regularly purge their VMF of inactive vendors. When these no-longer-used vendors remain on the vendor list, dishonest employees with access to the VMF may be able to perpetrate a dormant account scheme by changing the address on the account to their own and submitting fraudulent invoices with the changed address. The good news is that there are several effective and not-too-complicated anti-fraud controls governing the VMF that, if implemented and enforced, will greatly reduce the organization's exposure to this type of fraud. The obvious one is to be diligent about monitoring for activity in dormant accounts and examining any such activity you find. There should also be an up-to-date and viable vendor coding system in place to ensure that dormant accounts are always flagged as such. The organization should also be diligent about shutting down the access accounts of all employees who leave the organization—*as soon as they are gone.*

The bottom line. Accounts payable is fertile ground for employees to perpetrate a host of different fraud schemes. However, before you become discouraged, keep in mind that there are just as many varieties of *fraud-prevention* tools and methods to minimize your organization's exposure to AP fraud. These tools are discussed later in this chapter.

■ Accounts Receivable Fraud

Sometimes known as "skimming," "lapping," or theft of cash, accounts receivable fraud occurs when an employee who is responsible for handling incoming checks or cash from customers or clients steals incoming funds—usually before they are recorded as sales or revenue.

In a typical lapping scheme, an employee with access to active customer accounts steals a check meant to be credited to the customer's account and then credits that account with a check subsequently received for a second account and so on, like a Ponzi or "pyramid" scheme not unlike the massive fraud allegedly perpetrated by Bernard Madoff, except on a much much smaller scale.

Similarly, skimming can occur when an employee simply steals payments from a customer and makes no record of the related sale transaction. The perpetrator steals sales receipts made in cash, often neglecting to conceal the theft or by simply destroying records such as cash register tapes.

Similar to skimming is theft of cash (sometimes referred to as cash larceny) which is endemic in the retail and hotel, restaurant, and casino industries where significant proportions of sales are made through cash payments. Common to these crimes are thefts from cash registers or from cash deposits. Concealment is achieved by either destroying register tapes or voiding transactions.

◄ **Case Study #6**

Robbing Peter to Pay Paul

Jones Maintenance and Repair Corporation (not an actual company) has customer accounts for several hundred regular clients for which it performs weekly or monthly maintenance, cleaning, and repair work. Each month the clients receive a statement for the work performed in the previous month. Every month, the clients send checks to pay their statements.

1. When Client A's payment is received, Jones's dishonest accounting employee takes it instead of posting it to Client A's account.

2. To avoid having Client A's next statement show nonpayment of the previous month's statement, the fraudster posts Client B's check to Client A's account.

3. To bring Client B's account current, the fraudster applies Client C's check to B's account.

The scam continues until someone accidentally learns about it or an audit uncovers it.

How could this fraud have been prevented? List as many controls as you can. Compare yours with those listed in Appendix B.

1. _____

2. _____

3. _____

■ Kickback Schemes

You probably have heard the term "kickback." But what does it really mean? Many kickback schemes are similar to AP fraud because they sometimes involve a dishonest AP or procurement staff member awarding contracts to a preferred vendor against your organization's rules governing competitive bidding or new-vendor approval.

This is often done by awarding the business to a specific (also dishonest) vendor who is permitted by the AP employee to submit invoices that are inflated, that indicate delivery of products or services that are more costly than what was actually delivered, or that indicate quantities that are greater than actual shipment quantities. (Sometimes the deliveries are never actually made.)

The AP employee next approves the invoice, which is for substantially more than the vendor actually *should* have billed, and the vendor kicks back to the AP employee a portion of the ill-gotten gains.

■ Inventory/Supply Schemes

Unless an organization is a service company with few or no physical assets, it probably stores and uses various forms of physical supplies and materials. Collectively

◄ **Case Study #7**

Kickbacks Fly When Controls Are Weak

Stuart Dabbs of Global Solutions, LLC, of Fenton, MO, was sentenced to 18 months in prison, ordered to pay a $6,000 fine for participating in an illegal kickback scheme, and pay $440,000 in restitution to Nordyne, Inc., a manufacturer of heating and cooling systems based in O'Fallon, MO.

Background. Dabbs was a principal of Global Solutions, an independent retailer of computer equipment and services. His co-defendant Kenneth Kantola was the manager of information technology for Nordyne, Inc. Kantola was responsible for purchasing computer equipment used by Nordyne. Between January 2000 and December 2004, Nordyne paid Global Solutions $5.9 million for computer equipment. Dabbs and Kantola agreed that Nordyne would order computer equipment that was invoiced by Dabbs and Global at fraudulently inflated prices or prices that intentionally omitted appropriate discounts. Kantola then approved the fraudulent invoices for payment by Nordyne. In exchange for the approval of these invoices, Dabbs paid Kantola a cash kickback.

Insult to injury. Since Dabbs was the sales representative for the Nordyne account, he was also paid commission for these "sales."

How could this fraud have been prevented? List as many controls as you can. Compare yours with those listed in Appendix B.

1. _____

2. _____

3. _____

---

these assets are referred to as "inventory," and they can include raw materials, merchandise in the process of being manufactured, and finished goods.

These assets are *always* desirable targets of dishonest employees. There are many ways for these assets to go missing.

"Inventory shrinkage" is the term used to describe the result of employee pilferage of physical inventory. These thefts are committed most often either by an employee finding ways to have the items walk out the door or by orchestrating a more elaborate scheme involving falsification of sales, delivery, or inventory records.

Example. It is relatively easy for a dishonest project manager or other employee with the necessary authority to submit materials requisitions for more than is actually needed to complete a project, and then steal the excess.

This type of fraud is especially common in the construction industry (both residential and commercial). Contractors simply order more building materials than they need and have the excess delivered to a buyer with whom they are conspiring or to an undisclosed location where they are stored until they can be sold—usually at a substantial discount from market prices.

Another form of fraud occurs when employees in charge of inventory falsify shipping documentation to make it appear that materials were sold and shipped to legitimate buyers. In fact the "buyer"/recipient is an accomplice or a shell company whose address may be the home of a friend or relative.

A similar scheme involves a procurement or purchasing employee falsifying shipping documentation to make it appear on paper as though delivery of an actual sale was made, but the delivery was diverted to the perpetrator's address or that of an accomplice.

Important. To cover up physical inventory theft, procurement, or dishonest accounting, employee accomplices sometimes falsify shipping and receivables records or write off inventory as obsolete, lost, or defective. This is why inventory is frequently a key factor in accounting fraud.

A precise and complete inventory valuation is needed in order to accurately report the organization's operations and to correctly state its financial condition.

There are numerous ways for senior financial executives to manipulate inventory numbers to make it appear as if the organization has more inventory—or less—on hand than it actually does, depending on the fraud objective of the executive.

■ Check Fraud and Tampering

Checks remain a primary method of business-to-business payments, with Automated Clearing House (ACH) credit, ACH debit, corporate purchasing cards, and wire transfers completing the list.

Overall, however, as the Association for Financial Professionals indicates, "Almost all organizations (94 percent) that experienced attempted or actual payments fraud in 2007 were victims of check fraud."[5]

To put the check fraud problem into perspective, consider the following:

- Check fraud causes $20 billion in losses every year (Nilson Report, a leading consumer payments research organization, www.nilsonreport.com)

- 1.2 million fraudulent checks enter the financial systems every day (Abagnale Associates, secure document consultants, www.abagnale.com)

- Attempted check fraud doubled between 2003 and 2006 to more than $12 billion a year (2007 *American Bankers Association Deposit Account Fraud Survey Report*, www.aba.com)

There are no statistics comparing the percentage of total check frauds committed by internal and external fraudsters. However, given that statistics for fraud in general indicate a predominance of internal perpetrators, it is probably safe to assume that with most types of check fraud the same applies.

With regard to *internal* check fraud, some of the common schemes described in this chapter are probably already familiar. However, keep in mind that check fraud is a moving target; the bad guys are coming up with new ways to perpetrate check fraud all the time. While some forms of this crime are commonly known, others are being improved, adjusted, or newly devised all the time. It pays to keep a close eye on developments in check fraud, because a new type of scheme can take any organization by surprise.

Throughout the descriptions of check fraud the terms *forgery*, *tampering*, and *altering* frequently appear. The check-related crimes they define are all closely related. But there are critical differences, familiarity with which helps detect many of these frauds.

Creating Forged Checks

The Merriam-Webster Dictionary defines forgery as "the crime of falsely and fraudulently making or altering a document" (as a check). Check forgery schemes are perpetrated mainly by employees who lack check-signing authority. The employee steals a company check (usually a blank one) and makes it out to himself or to cash; or he makes it out to a phony vendor or an accomplice and forges the signature of a person in the organization who has authorization to sign legitimate company checks.

This is sometimes easier said than done. It is true that many banks, and certainly most retail outlets that accept checks (such as liquor stores, grocery stores, or other organizations where scrutinizing of check details is not a high priority) would not notice if a fraudster has done a poor job of copying an authorized person's signature. However, if the fraudster presents a stolen check with a signature that looks suspicious to the employer's bank, the forgery may be detected.

Employees most likely to commit this fraud include anyone with access to blank check stock or with an internal accomplice who has such access. These typically include accounting staff, AP personnel, senior financial employees, bookkeepers, and office managers.[6]

Check Interception and Forgery of Endorsements

Some check fraud perpetrators prefer to steal checks that have already been made out to a legitimate payee, signed, and prepared for mailing or delivery. They intercept the check either before or after it is sealed in an envelope. After stealing the check, they change the payee by using the old-fashioned method—by erasing the existing payee's name and replacing it with hers either by hand—or with a computer. See Exhibit 3.1.

This is often easy for a bank teller to catch, because these alterations, like the one in the image below, often are quite conspicuous. And, of course, if the bank does not catch the forgery, whoever in your organization is responsible for check reconciliations certainly should.

Another way for insiders without access to blank checks to commit fraud is to alter the payee *electronically*. This typically occurs when an insider who has authorized access to the secure computer system that stores all payment data abuses this authorization, by accessing the system, changing the name of a legitimate vendor to a name that is similar enough not to be noticed, and uses a phony or old invoice number to generate a payment. (Of course, at the same time that the payee name is altered, so is the address, so that the check will go to the fraudster's designated address.)

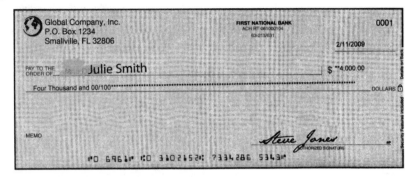

Global Company, Inc.
P.O. Box 1234
Smallville, FL 32806

FIRST NATIONAL BANK
ACH RT 061000104
63-215/631

0001

2/11/2009

PAY TO THE
ORDER OF ____ Julie Smith

$ **4,000.00

Four Thousand and 00/100••• DOLLARS

MEMO

Steve Jones
AUTHORIZED SIGNATURE

⑈O 6961⑈ ⑊O 3102152⑈ 7334286 5343⑈

Exhibit 3.1   Poor Attempt at Alteration of Payee

After the fraud is executed, the vendor's name and address are changed back and disbursement records are fudged to cover up the transaction. (This ploy is risky in many companies with tight disbursement controls, because such covering up is difficult to get away with. It is often easier and less risky to simply create a phony—shell company—vendor, falsify the addition to the Vendor Master File [VMF] and generate phony invoices to be paid to that "vendor.")

Check Altering by Inserting Numbers or Letters

The U.S. Office of the Comptroller of the Currency, one of several federal bank regulating bodies, explains that there are two primary ways that check fraudsters alter stolen checks by fraudulently inserting numerical or alphabetical characters before depositing or cashing them:

1. **Numbers Games**

   How it works. A dishonest mobile dog grooming franchisee provides a customer's dog with a shampoo, hair trim, and flea treatment. The charge is $49.

   The customer pays by check, writing "$49" to the far right in the box for the amount, and the words "forty-nine and 00/100" to the far right of the text line.

   The criminal uses the blank spaces on both lines to alter the check by adding a "9" before the numbers line, and the words "Nine Hundred" before the text line. The $49 check is now a fraudulent check for $949.00, which the criminal cashes.[7]

2. **Alphabet Scams**

   How it works. A company that provides cleaning and maintenance services to small and medium-size businesses is paid by checks made out to "Roberts Co." or "Roberts Company." A mailroom worker at one of Roberts Co.'s client companies steals one of those payment checks and uses a chemical solution to erase the word Co. or Company. She then types in the word Compton, and subsequently cashes the checks using false identification.

   Additional common check fraud schemes to beware of include:

   - **"Hidden check" fraud.** This is a ploy requiring a bit of psychological savvy on the part of the fraudster.

How it works. The criminal—usually a payments or other check-handling employee—submits a pile of prepared checks to an authorized signer for signature.

Included among the pile is one check made out to the fraudster or to a phony vendor or accomplice. The fraudster is able to get the forged check signed by the authorized signer because he knows from experience that because the signer is extremely busy he rarely reviews the details or the attached documentation of the checks he is handed before hurriedly signing them.

Making an informed guess that this will result in the bogus check being signed along with all of the rest, the fraudster outsmarts the signer by exploiting the individual's inattentiveness to the details of the checks.

Once the batch of signed checks is returned to the dishonest employee, she simply removes the fraudulent one from the pile and deposits or cashes it.

- **Check fraud by intimidation.** Senior managers and executives may choose to cross the line by abusing their authority to bully or intimidate payments employees into violating the controls governing approval of disbursements. They may request that an employee with authority to make checks do so without the normal documentation and approvals, implying that refusing to comply could cost the person his job.

  One infamous example of this conduct, though not specifically related to check fraud, was the case of now-defunct Sunbeam Corp. In the late 1990s, the home appliance maker was in financial trouble, and the board hired veteran corporate dynamo, Albert Dunlap as CEO to fix the ailing company. Dunlap had earned a reputation for turning troubled companies around by using drastic downsizing measures, thereby earning the dubious nickname Chainsaw Al.

  As the board expected, when he came to Sunbeam, Dunlap promptly fired huge numbers of employees and began aggressively selling the company's barbecue grills, electric blankets, and other items.

  But eventually his managerial excesses backfired. When legitimate sales did not grow to required levels, Dunlap intimidated accounting employees into making the company's financial performance appear rosier than it was, primarily by forcing them to recognize sales revenue for product that had been bought by wholesalers on a buy and hold basis. This is a tactic similar to channel stuffing where a manufacturer gives buyers huge discounts in order to move merchandise, but holds the actual shipments in its own warehouses for a month or longer before shipping and ultimately invoicing for the goods. However, the sales are recognized immediately on the company's books, thus making it appear as though revenue is higher than it actually is.

  As soon as this and other accounting violations were discovered, Chainsaw Al was fired, and Sunbeam's stock price plummeted.

- **ACH fraud.** Automated Clearing House (ACH) transactions are electronic funds transfers such as the familiar direct deposit of payroll checks. The good news is that losses from ACH fraud are considerably smaller than those attributable to check fraud. According to the Association for Financial Professionals (AFP), while 35 percent of organizations were targets of ACH fraud attempts, only 20 percent suffered losses due to such frauds, compared with 93 percent and 25 percent, respectively for check fraud.[8]

However, the ACH fraud threat is expected to increase as more and more transactions shift from paper checks to electronic ACH. This trend is being driven by the prospect of significant cost savings. The National Automated Clearing House Association (NACHA), an industry group of ACH network participants, estimates that a typical large company switching from paper paychecks to ACH direct deposit of payroll could realize per-transaction savings of $0.187. With a payroll of 100,000 transactions per month, annual cost savings would total $224,400. Even a small business with as few as 500 payroll transactions per month could cut costs by $0.352 per payroll transaction, saving several thousand dollars per year by switching to ACH direct payroll deposit.[9]

Similar savings are being captured in consumer bill payments. The Office of the Comptroller of the Currency reports that utilities, for example, save up to 85 percent per customer transaction when payments are made via ACH.[10]

Naturally, along with cost savings come new fraud risks. And while it is relatively easy to prevent most ACH fraud attempts, that does *not* mean that such attempts will not grow in number as the proportion of total transactions completed via ACH continues to increase.

This is how it works:

External ACH Fraud. Your company allows a few trusted, long-time vendors to debit your checking account to get paid for outstanding invoices. You arrange with your bank to put an ACH debit filter in place which ensures that *only* your authorized vendors can execute debits.

But a dishonest employee at one of your other vendor companies obtains your bank account routing and account numbers and, posing as a legitimate payee, initiates a fraudulent ACH debit that is credited to its own fraudulent vendor account.

Internal ACH Fraud. Instead of providing a creditor such as a credit card company or utility company his own bank account information, one of your own employees gives the creditor *your* payroll checking account numbers, representing to the creditors that they are from his personal account.

■ Travel and Entertainment (T&E) Fraud

T&E is a favored target of employees with expense accounts who decide to steal from their employers. In fact, T&E fraud is the costliest form of internal fraud at many organizations. Part of the reason is that it is generally very easy to get away with these schemes because implementing effective preventive controls continues to prove very difficult, in no small measure due to the virtually limitless number of ways that these frauds can be perpetrated.

Key figure. According to the Association of Certified Fraud Examiners, 13.2 percent of all fraud schemes are related to expense reimbursement, with the median loss per incident totaling $25,000.[11]

T&E fraud often occurs when employees feel that since they are traveling on business—an inconvenience and sacrifice—they are entitled to a little extra. Here are examples of common T&E schemes that have been uncovered over the years:

- **Falsifying receipts.** Receipts for transportation, hotel, restaurant, and other business travel expenses are easily obtained and recycled by employees either by forgery or alteration.

  It is all too easy, for example, to alter the date or amount on a "business meal" or hotel receipt before it is faxed or scanned.

- **Making multiple expense submissions.** When two or more employees dine together while on the road, dishonest employees may each submit a claim for reimbursement for their own meals even though the entire bill was paid by a single member of the group. Similar practices often occur with shared taxis, airport shuttle services, and so on.

  A related scheme involves a single employee submitting the same expense reimbursement claim more than once—expecting that the manager in charge of approving his claims will rubber-stamp the duplicate submission.

- **Claiming expenses just below the minimum for which receipts must be submitted.** If receipts are required for all expenses over $25.00 for meals, an employee may fraudulently submit undocumented claims for amounts for $24.99 or $24.95.

- **Falsifying automobile mileage expenses.** Since receipts are usually not required for use of an employee's own car for business purposes, the accuracy of these claims is difficult to audit.

  Important. Look for patterns of abuse. In one case, an employee was supplementing his income during a salary increase freeze by claiming mileage reimbursement for trips to the same location every week. The amounts submitted every week were exactly the same. When investigated by auditors, it was found that the employee had never left the building where he worked.

- **Falsifying approvals.** In the last case, it was also found that the employee was forging her manager's signature on the claim form.

- **Claiming for out-of-policy expenses.** A dishonest employee may test the waters by submitting a receipt for a personal expense incurred during a business trip. If the expense claim form is complicated, the processor may overlook an improper expense and unknowingly reimburse the employee for it.

- **Manipulating currency exchange rates.** Employees who travel internationally may intentionally use an incorrect or inflated currency exchange rate when calculating expenses in dollars. This fraud can be especially costly in volatile economic times.

- **Internal abuse of weak T&E anti-fraud controls.** Improperly established segregation of duties (SoD) for processing T&E claims can enable employees who process

T&E claims to falsify expense submissions by changing amounts or payees. They may either pocket the unauthorized reimbursement amount themselves, or collude with the actual traveler to exploit these control weaknesses.

- **Making "honest" mistakes.** An employee who always makes mistakes on her expense submission because "the spreadsheet did not work properly" is a prime candidate for extra scrutiny by management. In some cases, these "honest" mistakes can result in hundreds of dollars in fraudulent T&E reimbursements if not detected.

■ Payroll Schemes

The most common forms of payroll fraud are:

- **Adding ghost employees to the payroll.** As discussed earlier in this chapter, these are employees in name only. They are added to the payroll by insiders who have access to the systems that maintain payroll records and disburse payroll checks. Typically, the ghosts have the same address as the perpetrator or an address of

---

◄ Case Study #8

Wining and Dining on Customer Dollars

A large multinational corporation had major operations in Asia and other distant locations.

The headquarters-based manager in charge of Asian operations traveled frequently to China, Thailand, Vietnam, and other countries where the company had large projects. Because of his frequent trips, the manager developed personal relationships with several local individuals. He regularly dined out with them at expensive restaurants and submitted claims for expense reimbursement for "business-related meals."

The manager accumulated $25,000 worth of fraudulent expenses over four years. Then he began to boast to his colleagues about "getting away" with his expense abuses, justifying them by arguing that he "deserved" the meals because of his stressful travel schedule.

A tip from one of the manager's honest colleagues brought the fraud to the attention of senior management who confronted the offender and promptly terminated him.

How could this fraud have been prevented? List as many controls as you can. Compare yours with those listed in Appendix B.

1. _____

2. _____

3. _____

a colleague or family member. Occasionally, they are employees who recently left your organization but are in collusion with a payroll staffer who "forgets" to remove them from the payroll and receives a portion of the proceeds of the scheme from the dishonest ex-employees.

- **Manipulating payroll systems.** This again is a fraud that can be perpetrated only by individuals with full access to your organization's payroll operations. The fraudster alters the computerized data referring to her pay details—usually the salary amount.

■ Theft of Confidential Information

In today's complex, high-tech world, information is the fuel that enables employees to meet their performance expectations, runs the systems at financial institutions that process our paychecks, allows us to book airline tickets without leaving our computers, and a million other routine activities that must occur in order for us to get efficiently from one day to the next.

The good news is that while we try to get more and more done in less and less time, computerized information systems provide us with an invaluable way to organize, store, and secure the enormous volumes of information we receive and send every day and to communicate efficiently through such instantaneous networks as e-mail, instant messaging, voice-over-internet (VoIP), and wireless systems.

Because these amazing advances in data communication, storage, and processing are now firmly embedded in our daily lives, we have unintentionally created numerous, constantly evolving opportunities for criminals to steal our most valuable electronic data. Unfortunately, statistics prove that the biggest threat to theft of

◀ Case Study #9

The New Employee

At RBG Construction Inc., (not an actual company) with 250 full-time employees, the payroll process is handled in house by the bookkeeper, Suzanne. Due to an illness in the family, Suzanne is experiencing serious financial pressures. She adds "Samantha Smith" to the payroll at a weekly salary of $630.

"Samantha's" address is the home of Suzanne's friend. Suzanne pays her friend a monthly fee for this service.

For three years, Suzanne prepares, sends, and negotiates paychecks for "Samantha" until an internal auditor reviews the company's payroll records and discovers the scheme.

How could this fraud have been prevented? List as many controls as you can. Compare yours with those listed in Appendix B.

1. _____

2. _____

3. _____

confidential data is from insiders. As Eric Cole, PhD, one of the world's top experts in information technology points out, "While large organizations are vulnerable to this occasional attack, the vast majority of information thefts today are by insiders driven by financial gain or other personal motive."[12]

Employees exploit control weaknesses in your organization's computer systems to access and steal confidential employee data, financial information, donor information, and so on. They then make copies of the stolen data to commit:

- Identity fraud
- Cyber extortion
- System sabotage

The big threat is that if employees steal sensitive information and are able to extort money from an organization by threatening to make the information public over the Internet or, more likely, sell it to other cyber thieves to commit identity theft and fraud, *your* organization's customers and shareholders may lose confidence in management's ability to secure the organization's sensitive information.

◄ Case Study #10

Information Is as Good as Gold

International Service Company's (not an actual company) employee names, Social Security numbers, addresses, dates of birth, phone numbers, bank account numbers, signatures, and other personal information were publicly exposed after an employee took copies of this confidential information from one of the company's computer systems by asking the information technology (IT) manager to provide her with one-time access to the databases in order to complete "an important project."

The result. Several employees became victims of identity fraud after the info thief sold the stolen data to an Internet criminal who in turn created counterfeit identification documents, credit cards, and other personal documentation and used it to pose as the employees when applying for personal loans, credit cards, checking accounts, and so on.

It took *seven months* for management at International Services to learn of the breach and even longer to inform all of the individuals whose private information had been stolen.

The employee who perpetrated the theft was never caught because she had left the company long before the theft was discovered.

How could this fraud have been prevented? List as many controls as you can. Compare yours with those listed in Appendix B.

1. _____

2. _____

3. _____

■ Insider Abuse of Computer Systems

This crime is very similar to insider theft of confidential information, except that instead of stealing data, the employee uses the organization's computer systems to:

- Steal money via fraudulent funds transfer
- Manipulate computerized processes, such as automated payroll systems, to give themselves a pay increase
- Alter sensitive documents, such as employee performance review details

Important. In both instances—theft of information and the three crimes listed above—the offenses are usually committed through one of the following tactics:

- **Hacking.** Employees with exceptional computer skills break into your organization's computer systems.

- **Social engineering.** Criminals persuade IT staff that they "need" or "have special permission" to access secure areas of the organization's computer system.

Remember

Our reliance on computers, electronic communication, and the Internet to do our jobs opens up new fraud opportunities for dishonest employees. We must learn about these cyber vulnerabilities and understand our roles in preventing abuses of our systems.

◄ Case Study #11

But She Was Such a Nice Lady!

An organized crime ring, thinking that BR Publishing (not an actual company) was an easy target and had a lot of cash on hand, had one of its members— a charming woman named Sasha—apply for a job as a bookkeeper at BR's offices.

Sasha got the job and for several months performed great work and earned the trust of her co-workers. As the bookkeeper, she had access to computer systems and databases that were essential to performing her job efficiently. She quickly learned how the internal computer systems worked, and before long she was able to fraudulently initiate funds transfers, issue checks to phony vendors, and commit other internal frauds.

As experienced organized criminals, though, Sasha's accomplices knew exactly when to tell her to quit before the frauds were discovered. Once BP Publishing's management found out about the frauds, the "bookkeeper" was nowhere to be found.

How could this fraud have been prevented? List as many controls as you can. Compare yours with those listed in Appendix B.

1. _____

2. _____

3. _____

Note. This is *not* an example of collusion between internal staff and crooked outsiders, because in this case Sasha was not a legitimate employee of BP Publishing, but rather an imposter posing as an honest professional with the specific goal of defrauding the organization.

However, you should also keep in mind that abuse of computer access privileges is not perpetrated *only* by collusive insiders. In fact, as indicated earlier, the vast majority of computer-related information thefts are by insiders acting alone.

▶ Red Flags of Employee-Level Fraud

Now that you have a good understanding of the main kinds of employee-level fraud that can hurt your organization, it is time to learn how to spot the red flags of these crimes.

Key. As with external fraud, your familiarity with the tell-tale indicators of major forms of employee fraud will enable you to blow the whistle on wrongdoers before they can get away with too much. As a business professional, many of these red flags will help you detect potential fraud in your organization's financial reports and records.

To help you remember the many red flags of employee-level fraud, we will break them down into the categories that you learned about in the previous section.

Important. There are several ways that you and your co-workers and superiors can spot and report the red flags of employee-level fraud. In fact for many organizations, the most common way that fraud is brought to management's attention is by employee tip (see Exhibit 3.2). The reason for this is that a growing number of organizations provide training such as that contained in this workbook—aimed specifically at raising awareness among employees at all levels about the red flags of fraud.

It is also important to note in Exhibit 3.2 that internal audit is third on the list of ways that employee fraud is detected. Many anti-fraud professionals agree that this is because few auditors are trained to audit for fraud. However, as Chapter 6 discusses, this is beginning to change. Auditors are increasingly using what we call fraud risk assessments (FRAs) to determine the specific types of fraud to which their organization is most vulnerable. The results of these assessments, as will be explained, is a summary of the specific types of fraud that could occur at your organization, along with guidance on auditing for red flags of these frauds. This in turn provides clear indicators to management on how to tighten controls against the frauds it can suffer most from.

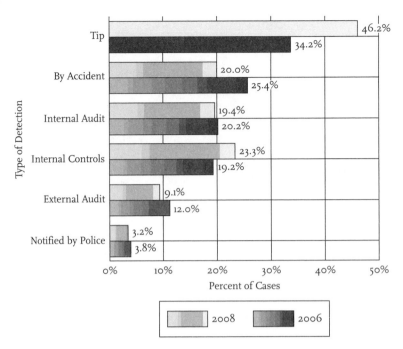

Exhibit 3.2 Initial Detection of Occupational Frauds

The sum of percentages exceeds 100 percent because in some cases respondents identified more than one detection method.

Source: Association of Certified Fraud Examiners, *2008 Report to the Nation on Occupational Fraud and Abuse.*

Remember

Without clear familiarity with the Red Flags of internal fraud, there is little hope of being able to find ways to stop it.

Red Flags of Accounts Payable and Billing Fraud

- Invoices have consecutive numbers despite being weeks or months apart.
- A vendor address matches that of an employee.
- Invoices are missing a key detail—such as date, address, quantities ordered, and so on.
- Invoices appear unprofessionally prepared.
- A vendor address does not match the address on the approved vendor list.
- Unusually high prices, which may indicate inflated prices for substandard goods.
- Unusually low prices: A vendor claims it is substituting a regular order with an alternate brand because "it is just as good for less money" (in reality, the price *is* lower, but the quality is *worse*).
- End-users complain about defective or malfunctioning products.
- The appearance of round numbers on invoices.
- A vendor's pricing does not match "regular" rates.

- A new vendor suddenly is awarded contracts, replacing an existing competitor that has had your organization as a customer for a long time.

- A vendor's address is in a residential or other unlikely area.

- The vendor's name on an invoice does not show up on your Vendor Master File.

- Prices on two invoices are within +/–3 percent of each other.

- Invoices are identical except that prices have the same first four digits

    Example: $259.66 and $2,596.77.

- A dishonest vendor sends two identical invoices except that the amount of one is exactly double the amount of the other.

    Example: $412.33 and $824.66.[13]

Red Flags of Procurement Card (P-Card) Fraud

- Unusual purchases made with a P-Card

- An unusual number of purchases for amounts just below the organization's minimum for requiring management approval

- Photocopied receipts instead of originals that are submitted with expense reports

- Split payments (an indicator of an attempt to circumvent purchase limit rules)

- Sudden unusual patterns in a particular employee's monthly P-card purchases

- Forged receipts

Red Flags of Vendor Master File Fraud

- Sudden reactivation of an inactive vendor

- New vendors showing up on the Vendor Master File whose names are similar to existing vendors

- Vendor addresses in the VMF match addresses of employees

- Key vendor information, such as EIN, full address, contact name, and so on that are missing from the VMF

Red Flags of Accounts Receivable Fraud

- Regular customers call to ask why, or complain that they are receiving past due notices despite having paid all invoices on time.

- Details of deposit receipts do not match credits applied to specific accounts.

- Amounts billed to customers are higher than amounts posted to the receipts journal.

- Sales increase, but receivables collected or deposits made are suspiciously low.

Red Flags of Kickback Schemes

- The same vendor is awarded contracts on consecutive projects.

- Product or service prices jump unexpectedly.

- A long-time vendor is suddenly replaced by a new one.
- Inferior quality product is delivered, but invoice prices are for higher quality.
- Invoices appear unprofessionally prepared.

Red Flags of Inventory Theft or Fraud

- Unusual fluctuations in levels of inventory or supplies for specific projects
- Unexpected shortages of supplies or incomplete deliveries (a possible sign that an employee is intercepting deliveries)
- Unusual purchases/deliveries of project materials
- Unexplained receipt of lower quality goods
- Sales that do not match shipping documents
- Unusual amounts of inventory that are written off as obsolete (may indicate fraudulent write-offs with new inventory being physically stolen or shipped to an accomplice)

Red Flags of Check Fraud or Tampering

- Blank checks are missing.
- Cancelled checks show signs of erasure or other alteration.
- Signatures are missing or appear forged.
- Vendors or other payees complain about not receiving payments (checks have been stolen and altered).
- Cancelled checks have fraudulent endorsements or dual endorsements.
- Cancelled checks show signs of erasure or other alteration.
- Bank reconciliation anomalies: Canceled checks do not match checks disbursed (or outstanding checks with numbers not appearing in bank statements or other payables records—a sign of stolen blank checks that have not yet been used).

Red Flags of ACH Fraud

- Unexplainable ACH debits from one or more bank accounts
- Requests from new vendors to allow ACH debits to receive payment of invoices (this should trigger an immediate review of the vendor's background, credit history, and references as it may be a sign of a phony vendor looking for a quick fraudulent payoff)

Red Flags of T&E Fraud

- Booking business trips but not taking them
- Falsified business meal, transport, and service receipts
- Submitting photocopies of "expenses" (can be a sign of resubmitting expense reimbursement claims a second time)
- Sudden, unusually frequent business trips (some could be personal/family trips)

- Absence of receipts/documentation for "business expenses"
- Failure to submit original boarding pass with reimbursement claim

Red Flags of Payroll Fraud

- Ghost employees are on the payroll.
- Former employees are still receiving paychecks.
- An "employee's" address is the same as that of a legitimate employee.
- An employee declines direct deposit of paychecks.
- Unusual patterns in hours worked.

Red Flags of Confidential Information Theft

- An employee uses a USB ("thumb") drive for no apparent reason (can indicate copying and theft of confidential data).
- Unauthorized system access attempts are detected by the IT department.
- An employee requests "special one-time" access to secure computer systems.
- Customers or vendors complain about incidents of identity fraud having been committed around the time they did business with your organization.

Red Flags of Insider Abuse of Computer Systems

- Reports by the IT department of unauthorized attempts at access to funds
- Downloading of prohibited Internet content
- Excessive use of e-mail for personal business
- Removal of organization-owned laptops for personal use or theft of confidential data

▶ Preventing Employee-Level Fraud

We must use our knowledge about the red flags of employee-level frauds to build an understanding of the numerous *preventive* measures available for reducing the organization's risk of being victimized. The lists of such measures are long. Indeed there is no such thing as a complete listing of preventive fraud controls.

Reason. As long as the fraudsters are thinking up new ways to steal, there will be an ongoing need for *new* updated internal controls.

The challenge. Choosing the *right* controls to minimize specific fraud risks.

To help in choosing the right preventive measures to implement, there is the fraud risk assessment (FRA). Chapter 6 shows exactly how to conduct an FRA and how it can make the job of formulating, implementing, and maintaining good preventive controls very efficient. For now, review the lists below of proven, *essential* preventive controls in the many business processes and procedures.

Recommended. Print out the following checklists of preventive controls and use them as a basic guide to build additional ones . . . and to help you fine-tune your controls once you've completed your FRA.

Note. These checklists are *not* comprehensive. Additional controls may be needed to minimize risk.

■ Accounts Payable Fraud-Prevention Checklist

Unlike most other categories of internal employee-level fraud, AP fraud seems to impact a wide range of processes and procedures. From check disbursements to vendor approval to inventory management and more, your AP function bears a heavy burden when it comes to fraud fighting. The following controls may make the job easier:

■ **Implement and enforce official *written* purchasing policies and procedures.** This is often easier said than done. However, after learning where your organization's specific fraud risks are, which you will be able to do after conducting an FRA (see Chapter 6), this challenge will become much easier. Suffice it to say now that your organization's purchasing and AP prevention policies must comprise a series of controls aimed at establishing and maintaining adequate segregation of duties (SoD) in addition to most of the preventive measures listed below.

■ **Implement clear and stringent SoD.** This anti-fraud control is critical *throughout* the organization, but especially in AP. Generally, it requires that two or more finance-related responsibilities that could together enable a single employee to circumvent anti-fraud controls be separated among individuals in such a way that minimizes the risk of such abuse. For example, ensuring that an AP staff member who is responsible for invoice approval does not also approve cash disbursements is essential to reducing the chances of a dishonest AP employee getting away with a phony invoice or shell company scheme.

Similarly, separating the main duties comprising the AP process from the key responsibility of reconciling bank accounts is equally critical for preventing many internal AP frauds.

■ **Establish specific levels of authority indicating who is permitted to approve purchases** and other business transactions, **for what items**, and **for what amount.** The term for this measure is Delegation of Authority (DoA). In the context of payments fraud prevention, it is best defined as a company-wide policy that establishes signature authority by level or position within the organization— with officers and employees who delegate their authority remaining responsible for monitoring and reviewing the actions of those to whom authority has been granted.

Helpful. Some organizations also have a finance manager approve expenditures for amounts above an operational manager's approval level. This effective anti-fraud control is referred to as the "double key" method.

For a view of how DoA works in real life, the following is an excerpt from the *Signature Authority* segment of the *Business and Financial Policies and Procedures Manual* of the University of Illinois:

A signature authorization form must be on file in the Office of Business and Financial Services for:

All deans, directors, unit heads, and administrative officers

Other employees who may be authorized to enter, review or approve financial documents

The delegation of paper document and electronic signature authority by administrative officers must be in writing and on the Signature Authorization Form. Individuals are authorized to certify and approve University business transactions only when given that authority through the Signature Authorization Form. This form formally delegates and authorizes signatures (manual and electronic) for certifying and approving individuals. Individuals are authorized to view, enter, update, and disseminate data only as required in the course of conducting University business. Individuals that have authorized signatures should read and understand the implicit representations of their signatures.

The signature authorization form currently contains:

The name, title, University Identification Number (UIN), phone number, department name, address, and mail code of the person being delegated;

The kind of forms for which the person is authorized to sign, including dollar limits, Banner Chart information as requested;

Current payroll system authorizations for Electronic Standard Time Report (ESTR) and Electronic Change of Status (ECOS) until the Banner Human Resources/Payroll module is implemented in January 2004;

Additional contact information for Banner Finance, Webcat, and P-Card system authorizations;

The signatures of the person authorized and the person delegating authority; and

An expiration date for the signature authorization.

A Web-based form incorporating Banner authorizations will eventually replace the current Signature Authorization Form when all Banner modules are fully implemented.

Approvals

The campus unit head and administrative officer request that the employee be authorized to sign documents and verify that the signature is real. The signature authorization form is approved by the Comptroller or delegate. No other approvals are required. The campus Assistant Vice President for Business and Finance is delegated the authority to approve signature authorizations and may further delegate that authority:

The campus Assistant Vice President for Business and Finance or delegate:

Must approve signature authorization forms before the signature or electronic approval can be honored.

Must be notified in writing to revoke approval authorization of employees who transfer to new departments or terminate employment.

■ Specific Employee-Level AP Fraud Controls Checklist

In addition to these general SoD and DoA controls, it is essential that effective controls over *specific* AP-related processes be in place. The actual controls contained in this category vary from organization to organization. And, importantly, continuous monitoring of the effectiveness of *all* AP anti-fraud controls must be delegated to a responsible manager who must be held accountable for the sound implementation and effective functioning of these measures.

Here is a list of specific internal AP fraud-prevention measures to consider implementing in your organization:

- Require approval of all purchase requests over a specified amount.

- Establish and maintain tight controls over your approved-vendor list (Vendor Master File). This includes establishing efficient vendor coding standards and monitoring for consistent adherence to them. Select a sample of vendor master records created and trace information to your vendor coding form to verify proper authorization of all additions and deletions of vendors or changes to existing vendor data.

- Avoid having people who are authorized to approve purchases also make changes to the approved vendor list.

- Require competitive bids for all purchases over a certain amount. Monitor the bidding process carefully to screen for potential bribery or kickback schemes that dishonest insiders may be perpetrating to circumvent the bidding process.

- Prohibit purchasing employees from accepting gifts valued at more than the organization's policy limit from vendors.

- Enforce monitoring for duplicate invoices.

- Manually review all unmatched open POs, receiving reports, and invoices.

- Immediately document all purchasing databases and shipping documents with details of goods received.

- Send all shipping documents and signed receipts for goods to AP within one business day.

- Never pay for partial shipments.[14]

- Require W-9 - EIN/TIN matching for all new vendors to verify that these entities are in fact who or what they say they are.

- Conduct a periodic Vendor Master File clean up to flag duplicate vendors.

- Investigate multiple vendors with the same name but operating from different addresses. This could be an indicator of an employee fraudulently altering the legitimate address of a vendor in order to have checks sent to the address she controls.

- Review any invoices that have been paid without a PO reference.

- Conduct a vendor audit if a billing, shell company, straw vendor, or kickback scheme is suspected. Your right to conduct such an audit at your discretion should be included in *all* contracts with outside suppliers.

According to well-known CPA and anti-fraud consulting firm, McGovern & Greene, LLP, vendor audits work best if you first do general due diligence on the vendor (assuming you have not done so recently in the process of negotiating a new contract with the vendor). Search public records, Dun & Bradstreet, the Internet, and other public sources to learn as much as possible about the company and its principals.

In addition, suggests McGovern & Greene, "prior to the vendor audit, a detailed forensic examination of the vendor's documents [currently] in [your organization's] possessions [should be] performed. The examination [should focus] on errors, anomalies, or other irregularities contained in these documents. . . . Circumstantial evidence may be found during [this] examination."[15]

Fortunately, the availability of such affordable audit software as ACL and IDEA greatly simplifies and streamlines the review of documents for anomalies that could be indicators of vendor fraud.

If sufficient evidence of an at-risk vendor has been found through an automated forensic document examination, conduct the following steps:

1. Research state incorporation records. This is a good Website to use: www.llrx .com/columns/roundup29.htm.

2. Check to verify if the address is in the same area code.

3. Pull invoices, POs, receiving documentation, and packing slips to check for anomalies.

4. Trace documentation back to the original contract to ensure that everything matches.

5. Call the phone number provided by the vendor to see if a business employee answers.

6. Use Google maps to determine if the address is a residential address.

7. Use a vendor profile form to see if it will be returned and completed with the requested information. For an example of a vendor profile form, see Exhibit 3.3.

8. Validate the Vendor Master File against the employee master on an annual basis to determine if there are employees posing as vendors.

■ P-Card Fraud-Prevention Checklist

Keep in mind that much if not most P-card fraud is perpetrated by outsiders who illegally obtain card numbers, expiration dates, and other data needed to create counterfeit cards. Consult with your organization's IT department about securing this critical data. While recent history indicates that many of the information breaches that have resulted in theft of cardholder data have targeted large retail chains, universities, and government agencies, there is little you can do to lock down the P-card data stored by these organizations when employees use their cards to make purchases. However, it is not uncommon for *insiders* with access to this data to steal it and sell it to outsiders who then either resell it or use it to produce counterfeit cards and use them to make fraudulent purchases.

Key lesson. Ensure that your internal information security measures are as rigorous as possible. It may pay to retain an outside information security consultant to evaluate your organization's overall defenses against cyber attack and to remedy at least any major weaknesses in your defenses.

Internal P-card Fraud-Prevention. As indicated earlier, there is no doubt that some employees who are authorized to use the organization's purchasing cards will succumb to the temptation to use the cards for personal purchases.

To minimize losses from internal abuse:

- Establish a detailed policy spelling out exactly what is permitted and especially what is *not* with regard to use of company P-cards. The policy should include limits on amounts of individual purchases as well as all requirements for transaction documentation and claim or expense report submission.

- Train all employees who are newly issued P-cards in the details of your organization's P-card policy, including disciplinary and punitive policies for committing P-card fraud.

- Require an *original* itemized receipt for each transaction. This should be a merchant-produced document that records the key details for each item purchased, including:
  - Quantities
  - Price per unit
  - Description of goods or services purchased
  - Total charge amount
  - Date of purchase
  - Merchant's name and address

  Important. Instruct employees to *ask* the merchant for a detailed receipt if one is not provided. Many merchants will also reprint a receipt that has been lost.

  Require cardholders to turn in their reimbursement claims and accompanying receipts promptly after they return from a trip. All receipts should be accounted for when the billing cycle ends. In addition, you should:

- Require cardholders to provide a business purpose for each transaction.

- Require cardholders to review and sign the monthly statements (assuming that the statements are sent to them rather than to your organization).

  Aim. To identify any purchases that cardholders did not make and for which there is no supporting receipt or other documentation. This can be a sign that the card was swiped by a retail employee. It is a common activity whereby employees use a handheld device referred to as a "wedge" to swipe customer credit cards and thereby have the card data recorded from the magnetic stripe onto the wedge's memory device. The data is later sold to a credit card criminal or used by the employee to create counterfeit cards with which to make fraudulent purchases.

- Require itemized receipts for all purchases, even if the merchandise was subsequently returned to the vendor.

- Require the manager in charge of approving and signing employee P-card reimbursement claims or expense reports to carefully review prior to signing, all documentation in order to verify:
  - Appropriateness of transactions
  - Correct cost center and account
  - Complete supporting documentation
  - Cardholder signature
- Require managers to review any transactions identified by AP staff as unusual to determine if they are legitimate.
- Remind employees that if anyone is found to have committed fraud, their card will be canceled, they will be subject to disciplinary action up to and including termination, and they may be prosecuted for criminal activity to the full extent of the law.

■ Accounts Receivable Fraud-Prevention Checklist

Management sometimes underestimates the risk of fraud in the area of accounts receivable. That can be a mistake. As such, the following controls are essential for most organizations:

- Double-check all sales records—to deter nonrecording of sales when incoming payments are stolen.
- Monitor for accurate recording of amount, date, and account of all transactions.
- Enforce access restrictions to automated accounting systems.
- Enforce independent reconciliation of all receivables records.
- Ensure that mail is not opened by anyone with access to the organization's accounting system.

■ Kickback Scheme Prevention Checklist

Kickback schemes have been known to go undetected for several years, which probably means that the victim organizations lacked some if not most of the following anti-kickback controls:

- Enforce segregation of duties (SoD) by ensuring that different employees handle the following duties: vendor approval, purchase requisitions, purchase approval, receiving/shipping, and payment.
- Implement job rotation. Do not permit the same purchasing staff to deal with the same vendors for long periods.
- Conduct detailed reviews of purchasing/procurement records to detect unusual pricing for certain vendors—*before* payment is made.
- Enforce consistent adherence to competitive bidding rules. If controls governing this process are weak or lacking, procurement staff have every opportunity to engage in kickback schemes with favored contractors or vendors.

- Immediately investigate any changes in vendors who have been working with your organization for a long time. A dishonest employee may be attempting to replace them with a new vendor who is willing to pay kickbacks in exchange for being awarded the organization's business.

■ Inventory Theft and Fraud-Prevention Checklist

Some of the most brazen corporate scandals have involved manipulation of inventory records. To protect your organization against these costly crimes:

- Enforce matching of all PO or requisition documentation with delivery documentation, and immediately investigate all anomalies.
- Check weekly—or daily—all supply/materials/inventory storage facilities to monitor for missing items.
- Implement/enforce proper inventory counting (manual or computerized).
- Implement appropriate anti-fraud inventory accounting procedures (these will vary depending on the organization and its income/delivery of physical materials).

■ Check Fraud-Prevention Checklist

According to banking and financial research organizations, checks are being gradually replaced by electronic payments. Currently, that trend is most accelerated in the consumer sector. Thus, according to AFP's *Electronic Payments Survey,* " . . . the majority of business-to-business (B2B) payments continue to be made by check."[16] As such, it is prudent to ensure that your organization does not overlook any of the following critical prevention measures:

- Secure all checks used by AP staff and enforce dual control of check stock.
- Keep keys to the check storage off premises.
- Ensure that all checks used by AP are consecutively numbered.
- Enforce levels of check-signing authority (see DoA above)—including when dual signatures are required.
- Permit no checks to be signed without required supporting documentation (that is, requisition form, invoice, PO, statement).
- Enforce full monthly reconciliation of all AP checking account(s) by a manager who does not have access to checks, signature plates, or AP software.
- Store unprinted check stock in a locked filing cabinet *under dual control*—where two locks are on the cabinet and two different people each hold one of the keys. Store check signature plates same way (to prevent collusion with outsiders).
- Secure boxes of unopened check stock. Avoid ordering too many blank checks at a time.
- Enforce check limits. These serve as a stop-loss control over cash disbursements.
- Always, always, always use positive pay, payee positive pay, reverse positive pay or a combination of the three.

- Conduct prompt bank reconciliations to ensure that any newly initiated check fraud schemes are quickly detected and stopped.
- Ensure that all payables are mailed without delay—to prevent interception by dishonest insiders.

■ ACH Fraud-Prevention Checklist

As mentioned above, paper checks are still the standard form of business-to-business payments transactions. However, many experts predict that the trend toward greater ACH use that has occurred in consumer payments will eventually migrate to the corporate sector as well. Even if your organization makes only limited use of the ACH system, these controls are important for minimizing your risk of fraud:

Implement ACH debit blocks on all accounts from which you permit *no* ACH debits:

- Use ACH debit filters where appropriate.
- Use ACH positive pay.
- Never authorize a vendor to debit your account via ACH *unless* you have received an ACH debit application from them that includes:
  - A voided company check with all necessary bank account numbers
  - DBA name if applicable
  - Phone number
  - Bank name
  - Bank address
  - An authorized company manager's signature
- Never comply with an approved ACH vendor's request to be paid from an account other than the one approved for ACH debit.

■ T&E Fraud-Prevention Checklist

Unfortunately, T&E is an area where the opportunities to steal are virtually limitless and the temptation to exploit them is difficult to resist even for the most honest employee. That is probably why the following list of essential T&E fraud controls is so lengthy:

- Require traveling employees to submit *actual plane ticket stubs and boarding passes* together with their credit card statements.
- Implement a T&E Code of Conduct with such rules as:
  - Personal expenditures are strictly prohibited.
  - Only authorized personnel may approve expense reports. Delegating this authority to another employee is strictly prohibited.
  - All T&E-related purchases must be properly documented in accordance with organization policy.

- Only authorized and allowable expenses may be submitted for reimbursement. Check with your department manager if you have any questions about the eligibility or the validity of a purchase.

- All dollar-value purchase limits must be adhered to. Splitting of transactions to avoid authorized limits is strictly prohibited.

- Prohibit up-front management authorizations of T&E expenditures.

- Prohibit cash advances.

- Require that expense reports and reimbursement claims include full descriptions of the business purpose of each expense, original receipt or other documentation, time and date, location, and exact amount.

- Be suspicious of rounded dollar numbers without supporting documentation—or with potentially counterfeit documentation—as well as a series of equal amounts claimed for a specific item or service.

- Have receipts cross-referenced to the expense report and sent directly to the processing group.

- Establish and enforce a minimum dollar level for requiring receipts in your organization.

■ Payroll Fraud-Prevention Checklist

The good news is that by now, most payroll operations have been fully automated, and the anti-fraud controls in place at third-party payroll service providers are generally quite effective. However, there are some payroll frauds that even the most cutting edge technology cannot prevent, which is why management must enforce the following manual prevention steps:

- Conduct background checks on *all* new hires (including references, credit report, and criminal background).

- Never permit hiring by a single person only.

- Conduct monthly reviews of payroll records to screen for unusual employee addresses (P.O. boxes, dual employee addresses).

- Ensure that the person who prepared payroll is not the person sending out paychecks.

- Conduct a periodic manual payroll distribution (instead of automated direct deposit), in order to determine if any checks are left over that might be intended for a ghost employee.

■ Confidential Information Theft Prevention Checklist

It cannot be emphasized enough that information-related fraud is rapidly becoming a threat of epidemic proportions. Even the best information security experts cannot keep up with the constantly evolving handiwork of cyber fraudsters. Fortunately, from lessons learned the hard way, there are effective information security measures that should be in place at all organizations.

For example:

- Clearly define and enforce data classifications. It is surprisingly easy to determine which types of electronic data should be made available publicly and which should not, and which types should be accessible only to specific managers, supervisors, and line employees.

    - *Danger.* Being too open with sensitive information. Some organizations put sensitive information on the Websites that should not be there.

    - *Solution.* Determine which specific types of data are top secret, which are sensitive and must be made accessible under strictly enforced access policies and guidelines, and which are suitable for public consumption.

- Use software programs that analyze anomalies in normal patterns of sensitive information usage.

- Hire professional IT security staff or outside consultants to configure these systems and train appropriate staff.

- Implement policies on how employees can use the organization's e-mail system and understand what is prohibited. Enforce access controls.

- Ensure strict management enforcement through automated monitoring of employee usage (this requires special software and skilled staff).

▶ Review Points

- Internal fraud occurs at two distinct levels of the organization: (1) the employee level and (2) the management level.

- Many internal frauds occur at *both* levels, but management-level frauds are usually far more costly than those committed by lower-level employees due to the comparatively greater degree of authority possessed by managers and executives to exploit weaknesses in the system.

- The Fraud Personality is defined by a clear set of behavior characteristics also known as soft indicators of fraud.

- The most common forms of employee fraud include kickbacks, AP fraud (including a variety of billing and sham vendor schemes), accounts receivable fraud (including skimming), inventory theft and fraud, check theft and tampering, T&E fraud, and payroll schemes.

- Theft of confidential information and insider abuse of the organization's computer systems are increasingly common and increasingly costly types of white-collar crime that must be defended against with the assistance of trained information security specialists.

- The first step toward preventing employee-level fraud is understanding and detecting the numerous red flags of such schemes.

- With a solid understanding of red flags, an organization can conduct detailed risk assessments to gather evidence of suspected frauds and put into place effective controls to minimize the organization's vulnerability to most employee-level frauds.

■ There is a virtually limitless variety of anti-fraud controls that can be implemented to minimize the organization's fraud risk. The choice of which controls to put into place is best determined by conducting a fraud risk assessment (FRA) that pinpoints signs of specific fraud vulnerabilities.

Business Name/Taxpayer Name (Exact Legal Name): _____

Federal ID Number/Social Security Number: _____

Parent Company (if applicable): _____

❑ **Domestic**   ❑ **Foreign**

Business Type:	**Officers:**	
Corporation	Principal/Owner:	_____
Partnership	Chief Executive/President:	_____
Sole Proprietorship	CFO/Controller:	_____
Individual		

Contact Name for Negotiations: _____   Telephone: _____
                                                        E-mail: _____

Contact Name for Billing Inquiries: _____   Telephone: _____
                                                        E-mail: _____

Primary Remittance Address: **Physical Business Address:**

Address 1: _____   Address 1: _____

Address 2: _____   Address 2: _____

City: _____ State: _____ Zip: _____   City: _____ State: _____ Zip: _____

Telephone Number: _____   Fax Number: _____

Company Website (if applicable): _____

Please attach at least three of the following:

Proof of Existence:
- ❑ - Corporate Charter
- ❑ - Recent Audited Annual Report
- ❑ - City/County Business License
- ❑ - Sales Tax Certificate
- ❑ - IRS Document/Notice

- ❑ - Federal Tax Return
- ❑ - Vendor Contract/Agreement
- ❑ - Product Catalog
- ❑ - 1099
- ❑ - W-9

Exhibit 3.3   Vendor Profile Form

Description of Business (or commodity code, i.e., SIC, NAICS, etc): _____

Please check techniques you are currently using with your customers:

      Evaluated Receipts Settlement (ERS)
      Electronic Data Interchange (EDI)
      Electronic Funds Transfer (EFT)
      Diskette EDI
      On-line Pricing Catalog

How would you like to receive payments? ❑ ACH ❑ Wire ❑ Check ❑ Other _____

Estimated Sales Revenue from [Your Organization]: _____

I hereby certify, under the penalty of perjury, that to the best of my knowledge, the information presented correct.

Respondent's Name: Respondent's Signature:

Exhibit 3.3 *(Continued)*

▶ Chapter Quiz

True or False:

1. The following are red flags of accounts payable (AP) fraud:
   a. Invoices have consecutive numbers despite being weeks or months apart.
      ❑ T   ❑ F

   b. A vendor address matches an employee address.
      ❑ T   ❑ F

   c. A new vendor is added to the approved vendor list.
      ❑ T   ❑ F

   d. A vendor's pricing is significantly higher than regular rates.
      ❑ T   ❑ F

2. The following are red flags of kickback schemes:
   a. The same vendor is awarded contracts on multiple consecutive projects.
      ❑ T   ❑ F

   b. A procurement employee suddenly starts taking long holidays.
      ❑ T   ❑ F

   c. Deliveries are repeatedly short but invoices are for the full order.
      ❑ T   ❑ F

   d. Vendor invoices appear unprofessionally prepared.
      ❑ T   ❑ F

3. The following are red flags of T&E fraud:
   a. Submitting falsified business meal, transport, and service receipts
      ❑ T   ❑ F

b. Submitting photocopies of expenses

❏ T ❏ F

c. Sudden changes in business itineraries

❏ T ❏ F

d. Requesting payment for expenses *prior* to traveling

❏ T ❏ F

4. The following are red flags of theft of confidential information:

a. An employee uses a USB ("thumb") drive for no apparent reason.

❏ T ❏ F

b. Unauthorized access attempts to secure systems.

❏ T ❏ F

c. A laptop computer is missing.

❏ T ❏ F

d. An employee attempts to change her system password.

❏ T ❏ F

Circle the correct answer to the following questions:

5. Which of the following is *not* a preventive control against accounts payable fraud:

a. Establish an approved vendor list

b. Prohibit purchasing employees from accepting gifts over a specified amount from vendors

c. Review all duplicate invoices

d. Eliminate all cash advances

6. Reviewing records for duplicate employee addresses is an important preventive control against:

a. Accounts payable fraud

b. T&E fraud

c. Payroll fraud

d. Accounts receivable fraud

7. Employee-level frauds are committed:

a. More frequently than management-level frauds

b. Less frequently than management-level frauds

c. About as frequently as management-level frauds

8. The financial loss resulting from most management-level fraud is:

a. Greater than the loss from employee-level fraud

b. Less than the loss from employee-level fraud

c. About the same as the loss from employee-level fraud

9. Theft of confidential information can result in all of the following, *except*:

    a. Cyber extortion

    b. Computer system sabotage

    c. Errors in T&E reimbursement claims

    d. Identity theft

10. Accounts payable fraud can be committed by all of the following *except*:

    a. Submitting phony invoices

    b. Bribing vendors

    c. Setting up shell companies as phony vendors

    d. Falsifying purchase requisitions

11. A kickback scheme is often perpetrated when:

    a. A dishonest employee diverts a vendor payment to his or her own account.

    b. Contract awards take longer than usual to complete.

    c. Invoices for more than the usual amount are approved and paid.

    d. Consecutive contracts are won by different contractors.

12. Check fraud is perpetrated in many ways. Which of the following is *not* a form of check fraud?

    a. Fraudulent endorsement of signed checks

    b. Altering the payee

    c. Depositing a check endorsed over to a third party by the legitimate payee

    d. Check counterfeiting

13. Employees who commit fraud often have certain personality traits known as "soft indicators." Next to each of the following, check "Yes" or "No" to indicate whether it is a soft indicator or not:

    a. Weak sense of ethics
      ❑ Yes   ❑ No

    b. Risk taking
      ❑ Yes   ❑ No

    c. Lack of team spirit
      ❑ Yes   ❑ No

    d. Refusal to take time off
      ❑ Yes   ❑ No

14. In addition to soft indicators, internal fraudsters often leave *hard* indicators in their trail once they have committed a fraud. As above, check "Yes" or "No" next to each item to indicate if it is a hard indicator or not:

    a. New, unfamiliar vendors on accounts payable vendor list.
      ❑ Yes   ❑ No

b. Check payable to a vendor is returned due to wrong address.
❑ Yes ❑ No

c. A ghost employee on payroll records.
❑ Yes ❑ No

d. Employee arrives at work wearing expensive jewelry.
❑ Yes ❑ No

15. Laura was a purchasing clerk at BWG Company. Her job included processing requisitions for supplies, services, and other requirements for all BWG projects. She was also responsible for approving vendor invoices, creating checks, and submitting them to her boss, Don, the Purchasing Manager, for signature. She regularly made out checks to a phony vendor, which she had created, attached it to falsified documentation and slipped it into the stacks of legitimate checks for Don to sign. Knowing he was very busy and unlikely to review each check's documentation, she regularly succeeded in getting the fraudulent checks signed. Circle the type of check fraud below that best describes this scenario:

    a. Forged maker scheme

    b. Hidden check scheme

    c. Altered payee scheme

    d. Check interception/forged endorsement

16. Bill, a regional manager in Worldwide Corp.'s office, travels frequently for business meetings and other work. He often pays for business-related restaurant meals and transportation services and submits legitimate receipts for reimbursement. On a trip to Worldwide's headquarters in California for a meeting, he purchased a necklace for his wife. It cost $98 and was bought at a local mall. Because he had become accustomed to having his many travel expense reimbursement claims approved and paid with no questions, he decided to include the personal expense in his regular reimbursement claim. Not surprisingly, he got away with this fraud. This type of T&E scheme is best described as:

    a. Falsifying receipts

    b. Claiming for out-of-policy expenses

    c. Making multiple expense submissions

    d. Falsifying expense approvals

Fill in the blank:

17. A person added to the payroll who is not a real person, but rather just a name and an address to which paychecks are sent is referred to as a _____ employee.

18. The most common crime committed with the use of stolen confidential information about an organization's employees, vendors, and donors is _____.

19. The most common crimes that dishonest insiders commit by abusing secure computer systems are stealing funds, manipulating computer processes such as payroll systems, and _____.

For the answers, please turn to Appendix A.

Internal Fraud: Management Level

As discussed in the previous chapter, internal fraud at the employee level encompasses a vast array of different schemes. Some are quite common—such as embezzlement, check fraud, and theft of confidential information—while others may occur less frequently at your organization.

The same applies at the *management level*. But also keep in mind the previously discussed rule of thumb that, while committed with less frequency than those at the employee level, virtually *all* management-level frauds result in the greatest financial losses. The reason is that managers and executives have more authority and therefore greater opportunity to exploit or override controls than those who work under them.

Important. Refer to Exhibit 2.1 and note that embezzlement—the most common fraud in most organizations—is committed at *both* levels. This includes kickbacks and accounts payable/billing schemes, which are broken out separately in the Employee Fraud side of Exhibit 2.1, because they happen most commonly at the employee level.

The following types of fraud make up an especially large portion of total management-level fraud and must be examined in the context of the comparatively greater authority that senior managers and executives abuse to perpetrate these schemes.

▶ T&E Fraud and Abuse

Dennis Kozlowski (shown in Exhibit 4.1), the former CEO of the major American manufacturing conglomerate, Tyco was convicted of, among other things, looting the company for his own personal benefit. To illustrate how managers and executives cost their companies much more when they commit fraud than their subordinates do, fraud prevention professionals and attorneys have often cited the $2 million birthday party that Kozlowski made for his wife's 40th birthday.

Though Tyco only paid one-half the cost of the party, and Kozlowski's attorneys argued at his trial that this was a legitimate expense because "business meetings" were being conducted, the jury was not convinced. The excessive use of Tyco funds

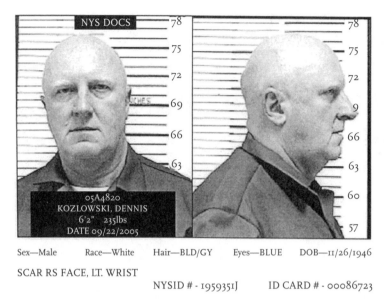

Sex—Male   Race—White   Hair—BLD/GY   Eyes—BLUE   DOB—11/26/1946

SCAR RS FACE, LT. WRIST

NYSID # - 1959351J   ID CARD # - 00086723

Exhibit 4.1   Former Tyco CEO Dennis Kozlowski
Photo provided by New York State Dept. of Corrections.

for personal benefit was an extreme example of executive-level travel and entertainment fraud (T&E), as it included the purchase of an ice sculpture of Michelangelo's David spewing vodka from his penis and a birthday cake in the shape of a woman's breasts with sparklers mounted on top.

Kozlowski is certainly a poster person for extreme corporate expense abuse. However, there are plenty of other senior executives out there who abuse their authority if only to a lesser degree.

This chapter's section on employee-level T&E fraud discusses a number of common T&E schemes such as falsifying receipts, making multiple expense reimbursement claims, falsifying approvals, and claiming for "out-of-policy" expenses. All of these schemes obviously can be committed at the management level—and are (usually with much higher dollar amounts). However, there are certain T&E rip-offs that only senior bosses can perpetrate. For example:

■ **Excessive expenditure of organization dollars for personal or business use.** The press had a field day with the discovery that former Merrill Lynch CEO John Thain had spent upwards of $1.2 million to redecorate his office, conference rooms, and the reception area not long before he was forced to sell the company to Bank of America due to monumental losses from the subprime mortgage meltdown. While this was *not* a fraudulent act, it was nonetheless widely interpreted by the public as a rip-off of the company's shareholders. Yielding to this public outcry, Thain, in a dubious gesture of goodwill, agreed to pay Bank of America back the $1.2 million, the expenditure of which he also admitted was a "mistake."

A related debate over excessive executive compensation—focused most intensively on insurance giant, AIG—was reignited as the extent of the financial crisis became clear. Again, while not illegal or fraudulent, paying executives multimillions of dollars while their banks or companies are going down the proverbial drain is at best an abuse of expense authority.

- **Company credit card abuse.** Most senior managers carry organization-issued credit cards. Large organizations have an especially hard time policing the use of these cards, and abuses are widespread.

One of the most colorful examples of management-level credit card abuse involved the former co-chairman of Wal-Mart Stores, Thomas Coughlin. At the time he got caught, it was found that Mr. Coughlin had run up nearly $500,000 in personal charges on his business expense account, mostly by making unauthorized use of his Wal-Mart credit card.

Here are some of the juicier details:

- Coughlin had 27 years of service at Wal-Mart under his belt at the time he committed the fraud.
- He was a close friend of the company's founder, Sam Walton.
- He rose through the ranks to become the Number Two executive of the biggest retail company in the world.
- He had an annual salary of $6 million when he was caught committing T&E fraud.
- According to court documents, he committed his fraud in part by having the company's Director of Development Operations, Robert Hey, use his company credit card to purchase Wal-Mart gift cards in amounts between $100 and $200 to purchase beer, liquor, food, and other items.
- Coughlin perpetrated a false billing scheme to obtain $6,500 to pay for his share of a private hunting lease.
- Coughlin initiated a false billing scheme to have Wal-Mart pay for service on his Ford truck.[1]

Lessons for all. Clearly, Wal-Mart's internal controls governing management-level T&E reimbursement were not adequate at the time when Coughlin was looting the company. Even if an executive intimidates a subordinate into falsifying expense claims, there are almost always red flags pointing to potential impropriety. Unfortunately, this underscores a challenge that all large organizations have: Reviewing the documentation of expense reimbursement claims can be impractical and cost-prohibitive by dint of the sheer volume of claims in a company as large as Wal-Mart.

Which brings up the critical issue of whistle-blowing. As it turned out, Coughlin got tripped up by an astute Wal-Mart employee who thought it odd that the top executive was using company gift cards to make merchandise purchases. The employee reported the transactions to management. One thing led to the next and after an investigation, Coughlin was fired and ultimately pleaded guilty to fraud and tax evasion. For the importance of whistle-blowing hotlines and other reporting mechanisms, see Chapter 7.

▶ Bribery

At the management level, bribery is one of the most common forms of *corruption**—especially within multinational organizations. There are two main types of bribery:

- Accepting bribes from vendors or contractors, bid-rigging schemes, and some forms of kickbacks
- Paying bribes to government or regulatory officials—to get things done

In the case of bribing vendors or contractors—known as "business bribery," as distinct from official or government-related bribery—the scenarios are well known. In its simplest form, a supplier or contractor who wants to secure a piece of business from your organization approaches an executive or procurement manager with the authority or influence to circumvent the organization's established competitive bidding procedures and offers something of value in exchange for ensuring that the desired piece of business is awarded. The "something of value" of course usually is cash, but it can also be free travel, use of a company airplane, or any number of other "gifts."

Important. In Chapter 1 you learned that such gifts are unethical but not necessarily illegal. In the above context, however this ambiguity does not apply. If a gift or something else of value is offered *specifically* to obtain favorable treatment, this usually constitutes illegal bribery—especially in situations where the individual accepting the something of value is a public servant to whom strict laws prohibiting such transactions almost always apply.

Key lesson. The distinction between a gift and a bribe is not always crystal clear. Many ethicists feel that a gift becomes a bribe only when the something of value being offered is, as mentioned above, given to obtain a specific favor. Others believe that *any* gift whether given with a specific desired result or not qualifies as a bribe.

A useful guideline is provided by Transparency International, a London-based group that researches and monitors international bribery matters: "The enterprise should prohibit the offer or receipt of gifts, hospitality, or expenses whenever such arrangements could affect the outcome of business transactions and are not reasonable and *bona fide* expenditures."[2]

Caution. Bribery and kickbacks are similar but not often identical. In some instances, kickbacks can be a *form* of bribery—where the dishonest vendor or contractor offers a portion of the proceeds of an illegally-awarded contract or business deal to the manager. In fact, the ACFE's Chairman, Joseph Wells describes kickbacks as one of the "broad categories" of bribery."[3]

Key difference. Kickbacks often involve ongoing payments by a vendor or contractor of a portion of the proceeds of a contract to the corrupt employee or manager who awarded the business. A bribe, by contrast, is usually a one-time pay-off in exchange for a specific favor such as awarding of a contract that would otherwise not be awarded.

---

*Corruption is a term referring to a group of related types of white-collar crime including bribery, extortion, conflict-of-interest, and acceptance of illegal or unauthorized gifts or gratuities.

Remember

In cases of bribery involving vendors or contractors, it takes two to tango—one corrupt manager and one corrupt vendor.

The second type of bribery involves paying bribes to authorities in order to get things done or cut through red tape. Someone at the organization's executive level offers cash or other items of value to one or more government officials or bureaucrats who have the authority to withhold necessary permits, authorizations, credentials, licenses, or other official requirements for conducting its business in the country, state, county, or municipality where it is attempting to operate.

All of these crimes violate state laws, although some states classify bribery only as a misdemeanor. Alternatively, major bribery cases are sometimes prosecuted at the federal level under the civil RICO law where, if successful, the plaintiff can be awarded treble damages and attorneys fees.[4]

Important. It is also a serious violation of federal law to pay a bribe to a foreign government or regulatory official in order to obtain or retain business contracts from government *or* nongovernment entities. Moreover, in more and more countries, such actions have been illegal for years but are just now being investigated and prosecuted with unprecedented rigor.

Unfortunately, as shown in Exhibit 4.2, the bribery of government officials to obtain business is *extremely* widespread.

The law that companies must comply with when doing business abroad is the federal Foreign Corrupt Practices Act (FCPA). This is perhaps the world's most

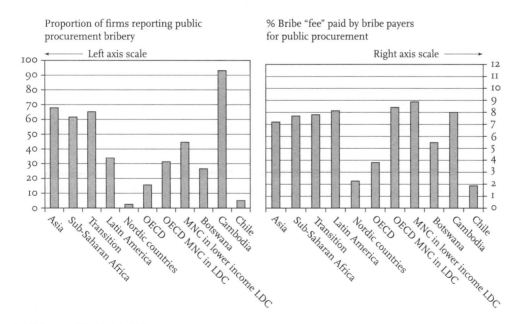

Exhibit 4.2 Worldwide Bribery

Source: *Global Corruption Report 2007*, Transparency International, www.transparency.org.

stringent antibribery law. It strictly prohibits U.S.-based organizations from paying bribes to foreign officials to obtain business or authorization to conduct business. An exception is payment to "facilitate" routine governmental actions performed by an official (commonly known as "grease payments").

Examples. Payments to secure basic services such as telephone, water, or mail; schedule inspections; obtain a permit, license, or other official document to qualify a person to do business in a foreign country; process governmental papers such as visas and work orders; obtain police protection.

Caution. Any payments to government officials *may* be in violation of the FCPA and, if discovered and investigated by the U.S. government, can result in hefty penalties.

■ The Greatest Corruption Story of All Time

The most stunning recent evidence of how companies are going to bizarre lengths to secure business in a tough global economy is the case of the German engineering and electronics conglomerate, Siemens AG. At the end of 2008 the company settled charges in the United States of having violated the federal Foreign Corrupt Practices Act (FCPA) by paying more than $805 million in direct bribes to foreign officials to obtain large telecommunications and other infrastructure contracts around the world.

Example. According to federal court documents, a subsidiary of Siemens paid over $1.7 million in kickbacks to Iraqi government authorities to secure 42 contracts related to the widely publicized Iraqi Oil for Food program. The illegal payments were concealed by falsifying the company's books and records.[5]

Further bribes and kickbacks were paid at the direction of senior Siemens executives in such countries as Argentina, Nigeria, Iran, Tunisia, Vietnam, and Bangladesh.

Although Siemens is headquartered in Germany, it became the subject of an FBI and SEC investigation in 2006 because it is listed on the New York Stock Exchange and as such is required to fully comply with all U.S. anticorruption laws.

Once the SEC began digging into allegations of dubious payments made by the company to secure lucrative contracts, the company's top executives began resigning *en masse*. By last year all of its top leadership had been replaced.

Under the settlement deal with the U.S. government, Siemens paid penalties of $1.6 billion, of which half was split between the U.S. Department of Justice and the SEC, with most of the balance going to the German government. According to the U.S. Department of Justice, the $800 penalty is the largest ever issued for violation of the FCPA.[6]

Following close on the heels of the Siemens settlement came the largest one paid by a U.S. company—Halliburton Corp. Some five years after initially announcing it was under investigation for allegedly paying bribes to Nigerian government officials in connection with a natural gas plant, Halliburton agreed to pay the U.S. government $559 million without admitting or denying having violated the FCPA.

Lesson for all. The FCPA is not a law to be taken lightly. Although obtaining business contracts in foreign countries is often dependent on payment of bribes, doing so is very risky, as the Siemens and Halliburton cases (among others) dramatically illustrate.

▶ Conflicts of Interest

A conflict of interest exists when an employee or manager also has a direct (but secret) financial interest in a company that does business with your organization, such as a construction firm, equipment leasing company, payroll service, or any other outside vendor. A conflict can also exist where a spouse or friend of the manager receives favored treatment in bidding for contracts.

Note. Many conflict-of-interest cases have similarities with shell company and billing schemes in which there is collusion between an insider and an outside vendor. The key difference is that in typical shell company/billing schemes, the shell companies are set up by fraudsters, but there is no real company. In conflict of interest cases, by contrast, there is an actual outside company in which the fraudster/employee has an interest.

Many conflicts of interest occur in the public sector where government officials with financial interests in companies they own or are partners in award government contracts to these entities in violation of the laws governing competitive bidding.

Examples of this abound. A particularly contentious case involved defense contractor Edo Corporation.

According to a 2006 report by the nonprofit Project on Government Oversight:

> A director of Edo Corp., the New York City–based defense electronics manufacturer . . . resigned his post amid allegations of a conflict-of-interest by a Washington, D.C. think tank involving a $7 billion military airplane contract. Dennis Blair, 59, an Edo director since October 2002, told the company in a letter . . . that he . . . resigned after the allegations raised by the public interest group Project on Government Oversight. Blair denied any wrongdoing. The public interest group said that it uncovered Securities and Exchange Commission documents indicating that Blair, a retired Navy admiral and former commander of U.S. Pacific forces, held several thousand shares and options in Edo, one of hundreds of contractors working on the Air Force's F-22A fighter plane program. The group said that Blair is president of a defense industry research institute—the Institute for Defense Analysis—that endorsed approval of a $7 billion contract to buy 60 F-22A airplanes. The group said that if the contract is finally approved, Blair stands to gain financially as an Edo shareholder.[7]

Key lesson. Most organizations have strict codes of conduct or ethics prohibiting any form of conflict of interest, which they try to enforce by requiring employees and managers in positions of influence to disclose all financial interests prior to employment and again periodically during their tenure. Unfortunately, this is not always successful, as shown by the following case study at the local level:

Brenda Belton's Conflict of Interest Scheme

Brenda Belton used her position as Executive Director of the District of Columbia School's Office of Charter School Oversight (OCSO) to divert money belonging to the District of Columbia, and money coming from the federal No Child Left Behind program to numerous bank accounts that she controlled.

Though this was a multifaceted fraud, a key part of it involved Belton's use of her authority by awarding seven no-bid school contracts worth over $400,000 to her own friends who in return paid Belton over $180,000 in kickbacks.

Example. In January 2004, Belton approved a charter school application for Young America Works, a charter school founded and run by two of her close friends, Brenda Williams and Nadine Evans.

At around the same time, Belton concluded a deal with Chillum Place LLC, a New York City–based private real estate group, of which she was a principal, to facilitate property purchases in Washington.

Red flag. One of those properties, at 6015 Chillum Place, NE, in Washington, DC, became the location for the Young America Works Charter School.

As part of her deal, Belton was to receive $5,000 a month from Chillum Place for five years—as long as Young America Works Charter School paid its rent to Chillum Place. Belton ultimately received $50,000 in payments before her conflict of interest scheme was uncovered.*

How could this fraud have been prevented? List as many controls as you can. Compare yours with those listed in Appendix B.

1. _____

2. _____

3. _____

* *United States v. Brenda Belton*, Case # 1:07-cr-00142-RMU (D.D.C. 2007).

▶ Misuse of Organization-Owned Assets

Misuse of assets is sometimes considered minor fraud because it often costs the organization little or no cash. That, however, does not make the actions acceptable. Such activities typically include personal use of:

- Organization-owned automobiles
- Office computers, cell phones, or other electronic devices
- Organization-owned computer software (by duplicating it and making personal use of it, a crime also known as software piracy)

- Service or supplies vendors such as:
  - Having construction contractors perform work on personal property at the organization's expense
  - Using organization-leased construction equipment for personal benefit

Caution. As with embezzlement and other frauds, misuse of assets at the *management* level differs from that at lower levels of the organization primarily in terms of proportion. When managers and executives misuse such assets as computers, contracted services, or vendor-provided equipment and supplies, the results *can* result in losses that are more than minor.

Example. The former governor of Connecticut, John Rowland, was forced to resign after it was discovered that he had diverted funds to a corrupt contractor who received $100,000 for work on Rowland's personal mansion and nearly $200,000 more for a contract to restore a state monument.

The result was that Rowland became the state's first governor to spend time in jail.

Remember

It is risky to ignore (or allow) improper use of organization-owned assets. Although such use may not result in a major financial loss, there is no guarantee that it will not. Moreover, doing so can send a message to other managers that engaging in this activity is okay.

▶ Fraudulent Financial Reporting

The problem of fraudulent financial reporting—commonly referred to among finance, accounting, and audit professionals as "cooking the books"—has a long history in the annals of organizational fraud. However it earned renewed notoriety after the Enron debacle, which was a book-cooking scandal of epic proportions.

Since Enron, literally hundreds of companies, government agencies, and not-for-profit organizations have been caught falsifying their financial records and statements.

Important. The most common motives driving dishonest executives to falsify financial records and statements are to boost share price, increase executive bonuses, conceal illegal financial transactions, and secure financing.

So how is fraudulent financial reporting perpetrated? In recent years, the most common abuses have included:

- **Recording false sales.** This is a tactic for inflating sales by simply recording nonexistent revenue. The purpose is pretty obvious: to make poor sales performance appear like good or at least not-so-poor sales performance.

- **Fraudulent revenue recognition.** Sometimes referred to as "premature revenue recognition," this is a tactic with the same objective as recording false sales: to make the organization's sales or revenue performance appear rosier than it is. But instead of just pulling phony sales out of the air and including them in the organization's financial records, this scheme involves recording actual sales from a future reporting period in the current period.

  A common technique for perpetrating fraudulent revenue recognition is called channel stuffing. It involves getting customers to agree to purchase goods but with the stipulation that they do not have to take delivery until sometime in the future—usually in the next reporting period. However, for accounting purposes, the dishonest organization records those future sales as current sales, thereby making the current quarter's revenue figures appear higher than they actually are.

- **Manipulating liabilities.** Also referred to as concealing liabilities or underreporting expenses, these schemes are perpetrated in a number of ways. For example, by simply neglecting to record expenses and burying vendor invoices, management can make it appear as though expenses for a particular reporting period were lower than they actually were, thereby making profits appear *greater* than they were.

  A related ploy involves classifying expenses as capital expenditures. This is a bookkeeping trick that essentially results in converting liabilities into assets, which is what happened on a grand scale when Worldcom improperly reported $3.8 billion in expenses as capital expenditures.

- **Overstating assets.** This is the flip side of neglecting to recognize or record expenses. *Examples:*

  - Failure to mark investments to market when the securities markets decline or when the cost of an asset, such as a machine or technology item, is greater than its current market value

  - Overstating the value of inventory—by failing to write down the value of obsolete inventory

- **Illegal financial transactions.** A common form of book-cooking is what is known as "round-tripping." This term is used to define transactions where neither the buyer nor the seller gains anything of value. For example, Company A "sells" $100 worth of goods to Company B in one quarter. That allows company A to record $100 worth of sales for that quarter. But in the *next* quarter, company B sells the same goods back to Company A for the same amount. But Company A is not worried about this "expense" because its actual sales are higher in the second quarter, and the phony $100 expense is unimportant.

  Result. Company A has manipulated its revenue for the first quarter by making it appear that it sold $100 more than it actually did.

  Important. These factors may not all directly apply to your organization now, but they *could* occur at any time. More importantly, they lead us back to the essential foundation of all internal fraud, which you learned about earlier: the Fraud Triangle.

◄ Case Study #13

The Great Buca Restaurant Fraud

Another example of how fraudulent reporting of liabilities was the case of Buca Inc., a chain of Italian restaurants that was investigated and ultimately sued by the SEC specifically on charges of earnings manipulation, which the company's top management perpetrated in order to falsely portray the company as what the Commission called a "growth company in sound financial condition."

The SEC charged, among other things:

> Beginning in 2000, [former Chief Financial Officer, Greg] Gadel preliminarily assessed Buca's financials at the close of each quarter to determine how much income he needed to "find" to meet Wall Street analysts' earnings expectations. Gadel pressured Buca's controller to "hit whatever earnings had been projected" by Wall Street. To fill any "gap," [top management] concocted a scheme to reduce Buca's costs through improper capitalization of expenses. . . . They merely took ordinary expenses, which are required to be expensed in the period in which they are incurred, and treated such expenses as capital expenses, which are expensed over extended financial reporting periods. The impact of such practice can be significant. For example, a $25,000 expense capitalized over 10 years amounts to a cost of $2,500 in the current year only.

> This scheme was effective. In eleven of thirteen quarters, Buca either exactly met Wall Street estimates or exceeded them by a single penny.

> However, in its restatement, Buca admitted that this fraudulent scheme caused it to overstate earnings by $12.6 million from fiscal year 2000 to 2003. The overstatement during this period was extraordinary—from 29 percent to 58 percent of earnings each fiscal year.*

How could this fraud have been prevented? List as many controls as you can. Compare yours with those listed in Appendix B.

1. _____

2. _____

3. _____

*Lead Plaintiffs' Memorandum In Opposition to Defendants' Motions To Dismiss The Second Amended Consolidated Complaint, *In re Buca, Inc. Securities Litigation*, Case No. 05-Cv-1762 Dwf/Ajb (Dist. Minn. 2008).

For example, Pressure to commit fraudulent financial reporting may involve:

- A need to embellish the financial performance of the organization.

- Potential loss of one's management/executive position. As Joe Wells of the ACFE writes, "Senior managers with strong egos may be unwilling to admit that their strategy has failed and that business performance is bad, since it may lead to their termination."[8]

- Need to meet board, shareholder, or Wall Street financial performance expectations.

- Need to attain specific financial goals to obtain financing.

The Opportunities to commit fraudulent financial reporting include:

- Weak internal controls over such key business functions as procurement, accounts payable, receivables, payroll, inventory, and so on
- Poor oversight by the board of directors
- Weaknesses in internal controls over financial reporting
- Absence of anti-fraud policies and procedures
- Lack of awareness among employees about the red flags of fraudulent financial reporting

As for the third component of the Fraud Triangle—Rationalization—fraudulent financial reporting can be "justified" with such attitudes as:

- *Poor tone at the top.* When management or the board display little regard for your organization's codes of conduct and ethics by maintaining a lax attitude toward controls, employee conduct, and compliance, managers can easily convince themselves that it is okay to manipulate financial records because "no one really cares."
- *Disgruntlement.* Managers who feel unappreciated by their bosses can easily convince themselves that their fraudulent actions are justifiable.
- *Poor communication or strained relations between management and outside auditors.* If management feels the auditor is exerting undue control over day-to-day finances, management may resent the perceived lack of trust and feel justified in exploiting opportunities to steal.

▶ Red Flags of Management-Level Fraud

The next step toward being able to detect, report, and/or investigate these crimes is understanding the tell-tale indicators of these crimes. Being able to spot reasons for suspicion is the essential first step toward apprehending a senior-level fraudster and taking the appropriate disciplinary or legal action.

Important. The following pages list the common red flags for each of the major types of management fraud discussed earlier in this chapter. However, it is also essential to be on the lookout for *behavioral* red flags of the costliest management crime: fraudulent financial reporting. *Examples:*

- Managers have lied to internal or external auditors or others in response to audit-related questions.
- Management places excessive emphasis on meeting financial performance or budget goals.
- Management is hostile toward or intimidates auditors—especially in defense of "aggressive" accounting practices that misrepresent the organization's financial condition.
- Top managers vocally express disdain for regulatory agencies and standards.
- Internal controls are weak, but top managers dispute this when confronted.[9]

You may want to make photocopies of the next few pages, which provide *specific* hard indicators (see Chapter 2) of the types of management-level fraud discussed in this chapter. Keeping them handy may prove useful in your day-to-day activities.

Red Flags of Setting up Personally-Owned Shell Company Vendors/Contractors

- Invoice addresses match a manager's address.
- A "vendor" does not answer the telephone.
- Approval of a new vendor is "expedited" by a senior manager by overriding regular controls over new-vendor approval.
- Invoices do not match deliveries.
- Invoice approvals are suspicious (a large number of invoices for the same vendor are approved by the same manager).
- A new "vendor" has an unusual overseas address.

Red Flags of Collusion between a Manager and Vendor(s) (via Kickbacks or No-Bid Contract Awards)

- Long-time vendors are suddenly no longer used.
- A sudden jump in complaints by long-term vendors about being suddenly excluded from bidding on your organization's contracts.
- Prices for goods or services suddenly jump.
- Shoddy merchandise is delivered, or poor-quality service is provided.

Red Flags of Management Theft/Forgery of Organization Checks

- Blank checks are missing.
- An unusual number of voided checks are recorded.
- An unusual number of checks are made out to "Cash."
- Checks appear endorsed by the same person (manager) who signed them.
- Bank statements show signs of alteration.
- Bank statements reveal anomalies in check sequence, payees, amounts, and so on.
- Canceled checks have dual or unauthorized endorsement(s).
- Vendors or other payees complain of nonreceipt of payment.

Red Flags of Management T&E Fraud and Abuse

- Booking business trips for personal use.
- Resubmitting the same expense reimbursement claims.
- Falsifying business meal, transport, and service receipts.
- Submitting photocopies of receipts instead of originals.
- Personal expenses are charged to your organization's credit card.

- Unusual patterns in a particular manager's monthly expense amounts.
- Repeated "errors" on expense reimbursement claims.

Red Flags of Bribery (Nongovernmental)

- Long-time valued vendors are suddenly replaced.
- Contract change orders lack sufficient justification.
- Delivery of shoddy quality merchandise or substandard service.
- Unusual offshore accounts are set up (usually slush funds for funneling bribes to overseas government officials).
- Prices for regularly purchased goods or services suddenly increase.
- Circumvention of bidding rules and procedures (including shortening of bidding submission time, imposing unusual and unconventional "qualifying" conditions for prospective bidders to meet, allowing individual bidders to submit bids *after* the submission deadline).

Red Flags of Management Misuse of Organization Assets

- Excessive mileage on organization-owned vehicles.
- An unusually high number of hours worked by certain employees (could indicate unauthorized assignment of workers to a manager's personal projects).
- Use of owned or leased equipment (computers, construction equipment or supplies, and so on) is not accounted for.

Red Flags of Conflicts of Interest

- Signs that entities owned by a manager or friend or family member are receiving your organization's contracts without going through the proper bidding process.
- Evidence of unusually high volumes of business with a particular vendor—especially a new one.
- Disclosure statements by managers are missing key details.
- One or more vendors begin to obtain an unusual number of consecutive contracts from your organization.

Red Flags of Fraudulent Financial Reporting (FFR)/Management Override

- Unusual/subjectively calculated drops in expenses/liabilities (misclassification of expenses).
- New, strange-sounding vendors (sham vendors).
- Unusual names of new customers (fictitious revenue).
- Sudden increases in volumes sold to specific customers (channel stuffing/ premature revenue recognition).

- Sudden increases in revenues compared to previous reporting periods and to industry trend (fictitious revenue).

- Unusual decline or lack of change in accounts payable for a specific accounting period in which sales significantly increased (revenue recognition or misrepresentation of liabilities).

- Unusually low costs recorded for routine processes or projects (understatement of expenses).

- Unusual budget excess or deficit at the end of a budget period (fictitious revenues).

- Frequent changes in outside auditors.

- Unusually high profits/margins compared to the industry norm (fictitious revenue, channel stuffing, or misclassification of expenses).

- Sudden increases in accounts receivable (falsifying sales).

Remember

Being able to detect management-level fraud at your organization depends on your ability to recognize the numerous red flags of the many types of fraud committed at senior levels of the organization. These red flags can be complicated and confusing, so reviewing them from time to time will help you to reduce fraud.

▶ Preventing Management-Level Fraud

Every organization has its own internal structure and management policies. Some are more effective than others in reducing the risk of management-level fraud. The best anti-fraud controls are those designed to reduce the risk of a *specific* type of fraud threatening the organization.

The challenge. Designing effective anti-fraud controls depends directly on assessment of those risks. How, after all, can management or the board be expected to design and implement effective controls if it is unclear about which frauds are most threatening?

The answer. It can't. This is why the next chapter shows how to conduct a fraud risk assessment (FRA). This is an important exercise designed specifically to determine the types of fraud to which your organization is most vulnerable within the context of its existing anti-fraud controls. This enables management to design, customize, and implement the *best* controls to minimize fraud risk throughout the organization.

According to the ACFE, the Institute of Internal Auditors (IIA) and the American Institute of Certified Public Accountants (AICPA), an organization's internal audit team must play a direct role in this all-important process:

> Internal auditors should consider the organization's assessment of fraud risk when developing their annual audit plan and review management's fraud management capabilities periodically. They should interview and communicate regularly with

those conducting the organization's risk assessments, as well as others in key positions throughout the organization, to help them ensure that all fraud risks have been considered appropriately. When performing engagements, internal auditors should spend adequate time and attention to evaluating the design and operation of internal controls related to fraud risk management. They should exercise professional skepticism when reviewing activities and be on guard for the signs of fraud. Potential frauds uncovered during an engagement should be treated in accordance with a well-defined response plan consistent with professional and legal standards. Internal auditing should also take an active role in support of the organization's ethical culture.[10]

Before getting to the nitty gritty of assessing fraud risks, it is essential to remember that there are *basic* anti-fraud controls aimed at preventing frauds common to virtually all organizations. Implementing those that apply to your organization is the first step toward building a successful anti-fraud program. They provide the foundation from which the specific, customized controls mentioned above can be formulated. The following sections provide a guide to such basic controls for your organization.

■ Anti-Embezzlement Controls

A. Shell Company Fraud:

- Regularly compare vendor invoices against the Vendor Master File (VMF). Investigate any vendors not on the VMF.

- Investigate unusually high purchases from a particular vendor.

- Adhere to all Delegation of Authority (DoA) rules for purchase/requisition orders/invoicing.

- Implement and monitor adherence to a system for checking for duplicate invoices. This may be accomplished in part by use of one of the popular audit recovery software applications offered by companies like Apex Analytix, Business Strategy, Inc., Connolly Consulting, PRG, and Audit Solutions; however, specific professional expertise is also required to manage this process.

- Enforce segregation of duties (SoD) in the approval and authorization of *all* new vendors.

- Set up a confidential hotline to gather employee tips about actual or suspected embezzlement.*

B. Collusion with Vendors

- Investigate all large purchases from a particular vendor.

- Monitor adherence to all authorization procedures for purchase/requisition orders/invoicing.

- Set up a system for checking for duplicate invoices.

---

*Having a hotline in place is imperative for both prevention and detection of all types of fraud—at both the employee and management level. For details on effective hotlines, see Chapter 7 and visit www.securityexecutivecouncil.com/common/download.html? PROD=72 www.deloitte.com.

- Enforce SoD in approval and authorization of all new vendors.
- Require approval for all vendor price increases above a certain amount.

C. Theft/Forgery of Organization Checks

- Reconcile all bank accounts immediately to prevent falsification of statements.
- Do not allow check signatories to prepare checks.
- Do not allow employees who approve invoices to prepare checks (or sign them).
- Mail checks immediately after signing.
- Harden physical security of check stock.
- Consider high-tech check printing with security features.
- Conduct background checks on all managers who handle checks.
- Enforce SoD on bank reconciliations (no signatories should be permitted to do reconciliations).
- Set up Positive Pay and/or Payee Positive Pay with your bank.
- Secure all checks used by accounts payable (AP) staff and enforce dual control of check stock.
- Keep keys to the check storage off premises.
- Ensure that all checks used by AP are consecutively numbered.
- Enforce levels of check-signing authority (see DoA in this chapter)—including when dual signatures are required.
- Permit no checks to be signed without required supporting documentation (that is, requisition form, invoice, purchase order (PO), statement).
- Store unprinted check stock in a locked filing cabinet *under dual control*—where two locks are on the cabinet and two different people each hold one of the keys. Store check signature plates the same way (to prevent collusion with outsiders).
- Enforce check limits. These serve as a stop-loss control over cash disbursements.

D. T&E Fraud

- Implement and *enforce* clear policies on entertainment expenditures—thoroughly detailing the types and amounts of permissible expenses. Your policy should include procedures to be followed for obtaining authorization to exceed the limits allowed. The action to be taken for violations must also be well-communicated.
- Require all manager reimbursement claims to be backed up only with *original* receipts.
- Have more than one person review claims (to screen for unusual expenses or prices).
- Conduct random/surprise audits of T&E records. Make sure all managers know you have this policy.
- Have the internal audit team review the T&E reimbursement claims-processing system—to identify possible weaknesses.

- Do not reimburse any claimed expenses not supported by original receipts (and original boarding passes in the case of air travel).

- Cross-check all dates of items submitted with the dates of the managers' business travel to make sure they correspond.

- Review two or three expense reports submitted by the same manager—to make sure the same items have not been claimed on multiple reports using different types of documentation.

■ Bribery and Kickback Schemes

- Rotate staff members who are authorized to approve vendors—every quarter if possible.

- Segregate the duties for approving vendors and awarding contracts or approving invoices.

- Implement a crystal-clear policy about the illegalities of accepting and paying bribes or kickbacks.

    Aim. To provide a deterrent to managers who are on the fence about committing these crimes.

- Monitor for the establishment of offshore or slush fund accounts that may be used to bribe overseas officials.

- Train all managers in the key elements of the FCPA and especially in the potential penalties for violating the law.

■ Abuse of Organization-Owned Assets

- Implement and monitor strict policies prohibiting this activity.

- Tighten record-keeping of all equipment and payroll (to screen for unusual hours being worked by certain employees).

- Tighten record-keeping for all equipment usage logs and make the employee in charge of record-keeping accountable for unexplained anomalies.

■ Conflicts of Interest

- Implement strict policies defining and prohibiting this activity.

- Enforce a policy requiring all managers to complete an annual disclosure statement detailing their personal financial interests in other organizations. Compare disclosed names and addresses with vendor lists to screen for potential conflicts.

- Promote your whistle-blower hotline to outside vendors, customers, strategic partners, and so on.

- Investigate any sudden increase in amounts paid for regularly purchased items or services.

- Investigate sudden changes from established vendors to new ones.

■ Financial Statement Fraud

While it is committed less frequently than any other type of management fraud, financial statement fraud is by far the costliest. According to the Association of Certified Fraud Examiners (ACFE), the median damage of a financial statement fraud is $2 million.

As noted earlier, financial statement fraud was instrumental in the collapse of Enron, as well as that of numerous other U.S., European, and Asian businesses. As such, the risk of financial statement fraud requires implementation of comprehensive and carefully designed internal controls, just like the other management-level crimes discussed in previous pages.

Challenge. Because financial statement frauds are usually committed by high-ranking officers of the organization, these people have the authority to override many of the controls intended to prevent such crimes.

This is one possible reason for the surprising fact that many controls against financial statement frauds do not work. Exhibit 4.3 shows that internal controls are less effective in detecting large frauds (incidents resulting in losses of $1 million or more—which statistically includes many financial statement frauds) than employee tips, accident, and internal audit:

Key question. What *does* work in reducing the organization's vulnerability to financial statement fraud?

Unfortunately, there is no easy answer. However, research does indicate that just because internal controls against financial statement fraud are not the most effective

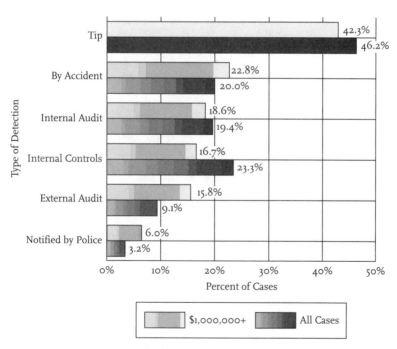

Exhibit 4.3 Initial Detection Method for Million-Dollar Schemes

The sum of percentages exceeds 100 percent because in some cases respondents identified more than one detection method.

Source: Association of Certified Fraud Examiners, *2008 Report to the Nation on Occupational Fraud and Abuse.*

method for detecting these crimes, organizations should not downplay their importance. In fact in the same report from the ACFE, it is shown that the percentage of organizations in which internal controls *were* the most effective, fraud detection increased significantly, from 19.2 percent in 2006 to 23.2 percent in 2008.[11]

Beyond implementing controls, there is ample evidence to indicate that organizations whose management teams implement and monitor a strong prevention environment are much less likely to be victimized by book-cooking schemes than others.

The term *prevention environment* refers to a number of critical top management standards and strategies. For starters, as Tommie Singleton, PhD, an associate professor and Director of the Forensic Accounting Program at the University of Alabama at Birmingham suggests, "The prevention environment begins with the policies and procedures of the entity, more specifically the policies. It is from the policies that internal controls are developed. It is from the policies that actions and transactions are determined to be unethical and it is from those policies that it is determined how fraudsters or violations of the corporate culture will be treated."[12]

Others agree. Christine Doxey, Vice President of Business Strategy, Inc., a consulting firm in Grand Rapids, Michigan, says, "It all starts with tone at the top. If top management sets a policy of 'zero tolerance' for fraud and establishes stringent policies that demonstrate that this is not mere 'talk,' the culture of the organization is well-defined to implement real controls that minimize the risk of financial statement fraud."

Singleton, Doxey, and other respected anti-fraud experts concur that the first policies needed to accomplish the zero-tolerance objective are those contained in a carefully-worded code of ethics. The code should lay out in broad terms the organization's commitment to high standards of business conduct and define the organization's *values* of integrity, fairness, respect, and commitment as well as specific ethics-related strategies. Specifically, the code of ethics should spell out policies such as those prohibiting acceptance of lavish gifts from vendors, offering or accepting bribes, and engaging in discrimination of any kind.

Important. An ethics policy is only the *foundation* for controls against fraudulent financial reporting (and against other forms of fraud as well). Ethics and compliance policies, while important, are not designed to prevent fraud *per se*. However, when an organization's top management puts into place an ethics policy that serves as *more* than just a means of complying with laws or regulations requiring the implementation of such a policy, the next steps toward *fraud-prevention* can be taken.

In the area of fraudulent financial reporting, these critical steps include:

- **Establishing a competent and independent audit committee**. In the big accounting scandals, one common characteristic of the victimized organizations was a climate of privileged cronyism among board members, which served the purposes of self-congratulation by a bunch of powerful people—with a bare minimum of time or genuine effort given to matters of corporate governance.

In fact, in the late 1990s and early 2000s, the culture among corporate boards was so bad that renowned U.S. litigation attorney John "Sean" Coffey, said:

> The Who's Who of the business, political, and social worlds were regular members of big company boards of directors. In many cases, board meetings resembled self-congratulatory social fetes with little if any serious "directoring." . . . The problem was that no one was watching. Federal regulators in the 1990s were stretched thin in the areas of enforcement and litigation. They simply lacked the experienced manpower to scrutinize potentially shaky securities deals and questionable corporate reporting.
>
> This dangerous status quo in the corporate finance field created a virtual license for corporate management to fudge financial reports to deceive shareholders and bankers, authorize ultra-risky securities deals, execute new and bizarre (and often grossly illegal) financial transactions such as "round-tripping," and to otherwise loot their companies, à la ex-Tyco CEO, Dennis Kozlowski with his multimillion dollar birthday party for his wife, courtesy, in part, of the company's shareholders.
>
> So corrupt was the world of high-finance during this period that whistle-blowers regularly went unheeded.
>
> **Example:** One of the country's largest not-for-profit organizations at the time—The Baptist Foundation of America (BFA)—perpetuated one of the biggest Ponzi schemes ever after its massive investments in lousy real estate went bust and it fabricated deals where friends of management would purchase worthless real estate with little down payment and worthless "notes" just to show profitable transactions on the balance sheet.
>
> Arthur Andersen, BFA's outside auditors, received numerous calls from concerned congregants but chose to look the other way for fear of jeopardizing its fat fees.
>
> This may have been one of the first examples of how a complete lack of professional skepticism can lead directly to a massive audit failure, not to mention the collapse of the client itself![13]

Lesson for all. Leading up to the Enron era, enormous institutions were run with no board-level governance to speak of.

Solution. Companies need genuinely independent and *vigilant* audit, ethics, compliance, and governance committees. These bodies must be populated by individuals with superior professional competence and experience and not because they happen to be friends of the CEO.

Key. These oversight bodies must also vigorously monitor the anti-fraud controls designed to minimize risks of fraudulent financial reporting. And they must ensure that all major senior-management level decisions—such as all multimillion dollar expenditures, deals with third parties, and other significant financial or accounting-related decisions are fully recorded in the minutes of their meetings.

Preferable. Have an independent outside consultant oversee documentation of the proceedings of all board-level committees. Not only will this provide a powerful deterrent to top managers who may be tempted to commit financial reporting crimes, it will provide shareholders and other interested parties with an independent view into the activities of the committees so that their performance can be monitored.

- **Continuously monitoring transactions** and business relationships between managers, vendors, purchasing staff, and others involved in financial transactions.

Transactions can often be monitored to screen for anomalous patterns that could be indicative of individually-perpetrated or collusive frauds.

- **Hardening physical control/security** of assets, records, and computer systems housing financial applications.

- **Reducing Pressure, Opportunity, and Rationalization.** The key for board-level committees as well as honest senior managers is to create a workplace culture in which the Fraud Triangle will have no bearing on the activities of managers in a position to influence the organization's financial records.

Steps to take

- **Reduce Pressure to cook the books:**
  - Avoid setting unrealistic financial performance goals for management.
  - Adjust (downgrade) goals if the economy or market conditions worsen.
  - Be sure that compensation rates are competitive and avoid excessive performance-based compensation plans.
  - Review and if necessary eliminate bureaucratic or other procedural obstacles to performance.

- **Reduce Opportunity to commit fraudulent financial reporting:**
  - Consistently maintain detailed and accurate accounting records—to eliminate lapses or sloppiness in accounting practices that dishonest managers can exploit.
  - Strengthen and sustain physical security of assets including blank check stock, cash, and saleable goods.
  - Enforce strict SoD for all finance-related management duties. Have an independent reviewer assess the integrity of the SoD procedures—to prevent management collusion.
  - Conduct thorough background checks on *all* managers.
  - Eliminate any exception clauses in accounting procedures.
  - Enlist and insist on audit committee oversight of financial reporting functions and controls.
  - Consider retaining an external financial reporting controls expert—such as a forensic accountant, Sarbanes-Oxley (SOX) consultant, or certified fraud examiner—to assist in developing, implementing, and enforcing controls of financial reporting.

- **Reduce Rationalization of fraudulent financial reporting:**
  - Establish and maintain the right tone at the top and promote a culture of doing the right thing. Not only does this establish an example of integrity for all employees to adhere to, it greatly reduces the temptation of executives to cook the books, thereby eliminating the need for rationalization for doing so.
  - Enforce a policy that attaining financial goals is *never* as important as maintaining integrity and adhering to high ethical standards.

Remember

Financial statement frauds are among the least frequently committed frauds in most organizations. However, they are by far the costliest. This is also why implementing effective internal controls for this type of fraud is usually the most challenging.

▶ **Review Points**

- Bribery, though widespread in the United States and around the world, is illegal, and violates most organizations' business standards and codes of ethics. All U.S.-based organizations are also subject to the federal Foreign Corrupt Practices Act (FCPA)—a stringent federal law that is being enforced with increased vigor by the U.S. Justice Department and the Securities and Exchange Commission. Record penalties for violation of the FCPA were imposed in 2008.

- Conflicts of interest are often easy to conceal during day-to-day operations. However, most such cases do have several red flags for which trained financial personnel should be on the lookout.

- Managers and executives are the custodians of the organization's assets. Misuse of these assets for personal gain harms the shareholders or owners *and* damages the organization's reputation.

- Fraudulent financial reporting often takes the form of four main techniques: prematurely recording revenue; creating fictitious revenue; neglecting to recognize liabilities; and overstating assets.

- Recognizing the red flags of management-level fraud is the key to detecting frauds in progress and to initiating investigations when they are warranted.

- The key to minimizing management-level fraud risk is building specially-designed controls based on the assessment of actual fraud threats to your organization. However, research has shown that internal controls against large-scale frauds are not the most effective way to detect such frauds. Instead, tips from employees, accidental detection, and internal audits yield better results. Nonetheless, internal controls against financial fraud must be continuously improved, as statistics further prove that the effectiveness of such controls in detecting fraud *has* improved in recent years.

▶ **Chapter Quiz**

True or False:

1. U.S.-based organizations are subject to the federal Foreign Corrupt Practices Act (FCPA).

   ❏ True   ❏ False

2. The Fraud Triangle has no bearing on implementing effective controls against fraudulent financial reporting.

❑ True ❑ False

3. Prematurely recognizing revenue and neglecting to recognize liabilities are *both* examples of fraudulent financial reporting.

❑ True ❑ False

Circle the correct answer to the following questions:

4. Extortion is a form of:

a. Conflict of interest

b. Corruption

c. Bribery

d. Embezzlement

5. Bribery typically involves:

a. A one-time pay-off

b. An ongoing payment by a vendor or contractor

c. A payment for submitting a bid on a contract

d. Persuading an employee to give out confidential information

6. Among the few exceptions to the strict laws against bribing government officials is:

a. Paying to obtain a tax advantage

b. Paying to obtain a required business permit

c. Paying for certification as a not-for-profit organization

d. Paying to obtain prompt telephone, mail, or electrical service

7. Gerald is a Finance Manager at your organization. In his financial disclosure he revealed that his wife owns a local concrete producer. But he did *not* disclose that she also owns a construction company. After the construction company obtains three consecutive contracts from your organization, internal audit decides to check into the ownership of the company and learns that Gerald's wife is the owner. This is a classic case of:

a. A kickback scheme

b. Conflict of interest

c. Identity fraud

d. Abuse of organization assets

8. Fraudulently requisitioning the use of organization-owned or leased vehicles for personal use is an example of:

a. Conflict of interest

b. Embezzlement

c. Misuse of organization assets

d. Asset misappropriation

Fill in the blank:

9. A possible red flag of check fraud is an unusual number of organization checks made out to _____.

10. A common form of travel and entertainment (T&E) fraud is booking trips for _____.

11. Excessive mileage on organization-owned or leased vehicles is a possible red flag of _____.

Circle the correct answer to the following questions:

12. Sandra works as a Procurement Manager. Battling severe personal financial pressure, she decides to steal three blank organization checks. She makes them out to "Quality Machinery Repair" and records the payments as "Maintenance." Because Quality Machinery Repair is a company in name only, Sandra is able to endorse the checks and deposit them in a fraudulent bank account for the "company" and withdraw the funds. This chain of events represents which of the following? (Choose all that apply.)

    a. Embezzlement

    b. Check fraud

    c. Conflict of interest

    d. Misuse of organization assets

13. Requiring reimbursement claims to be backed up with original receipts is a preventive control against:

    a. Embezzlement

    b. T&E fraud

    c. Misuse of assets

    d. Check fraud

14. Reducing Pressure, Opportunities, and Rationalization for managers is especially important to reducing the motive to perpetrate:

    a. Kickback schemes

    b. Fraudulent financial reporting

    c. Check fraud

    d. Collusion with vendors

For the answers, please turn to Appendix A.

CHAPTER FIVE

External Fraud: Protecting Against Dishonest Outsiders

Total fraud losses in the United States alone amount to more than $1 trillion, and the majority of fraud is committed by insiders—up to 80 percent of the total (see Chapter 1).

It is important to note that while *internal* fraud is more common and more costly than *external* fraud, the latter is still potentially very damaging. This chapter discusses the main types of external fraud, how to detect the red flags of these crimes and how to report incidents to people in your organization with the skills to investigate them.

Note. As with internal fraud, external schemes also frequently involve collusion between one or more insiders and a crooked vendor, government official, or other outsider. The majority of external fraud schemes are perpetrated by dishonest vendors or by dishonest individuals perpetrating phony vendor schemes. A variety of deceptive tactics are used to carry out these frauds, including social engineering and pretexting—terms used to describe what used to be commonly referred to as "conning." In addition, external fraud is sometimes committed by dishonest employees of the bank where you have business accounts.

Important. Do not underestimate the potential for your own customers to scam you as well. The following pages will show you a few ways this is done and provide you with tell-tale signs of such schemes.

▶ Types of External Fraud

Unfortunately, external fraudsters are notoriously clever when it comes to thinking up new ways to steal from or deceive an organization. Following are the most common external frauds.

■ Vendor and Billing Fraud

For most organizations, the largest group of external fraudsters is dishonest vendors. Over the years, crooked vendors have come up with a wide variety of ways to rip off their customers. Understanding the mechanics of these crimes is the first step to putting defensive controls in place.

Common vendor and billing schemes to beware of include:

- **Double billing.** These crimes are committed exactly as their name suggests: Dishonest vendors submit a duplicate invoice a month or two after the initial—legitimate—one was submitted and paid. As you can tell in Exhibit 5.1, the invoice will sometimes have a different date or a consecutive number (a clear red flag of fraud). But the ploy is based on the vendor's expectation that your organization's accounts payable processes lack adequate controls to screen for duplicate billing and that the second—fraudulent—invoice will therefore be approved and paid without being questioned.

- **Delivery of substandard goods at full price.** Some of the goods and services that your organization orders for completion of projects for clients, for its own operations, or both are ordered from vendors with which the organization has had a long-standing relationship due to good service, quality products, and favorable pricing. Other orders may be made based on competitive bidding.

    Either way, it is risky to assume that every vendor you do business with is completely honest. There are usually a handful that take advantage of lax controls in your procurement or accounts payable processes to deliver products that are below the quality specified in a contract or purchase order and then bill your organization for the higher quality—and higher priced—goods. The difference in price, of course, goes straight into the dishonest vendor's pocket.

- **Creating phony vendors.** As discussed in Chapters 3 and 4, employees typically have the necessary access to company procurement and accounts payable records that enables them to "hide" phony vendors among the legitimate ones.

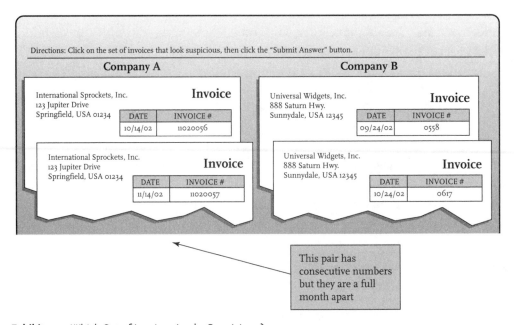

Exhibit 5.1 Which Set of Invoices Looks Suspicious?

However, outsiders have their own tricks when it comes to phony vendor ploys. The basic idea behind most external phony vendor schemes is simple: Create a phony company name—such as General Materials Company, register it with the proper state agencies, give it a phony address—either that of the fraudster himself or a friend or relative—and use a computer to create phony invoices with all of this vendor information plus a description of the items or service being billed for. Then sit back and wait for the checks to arrive.

If the targeted organization has strong internal controls in place in its accounts payable department, the phony invoices will be flagged and rejected as fraudulent. If not, the fraudster gets the payment and, encouraged by this success, will probably repeat the process using the same or a different vendor name.

- **Subcontractors falsifying records to misappropriate funds.** These scams occur when your organization hires a subcontractor with specialized skills or services to assist in completing a project for a client, or when a unique piece of equipment is needed to complete a project. The subcontractor's work begins when the invoices submitted to the project director are inflated or completely fabricated. Since the services being provided are unusual, your managers may be unfamiliar with the "fair price" for the services and simply assume that the invoices being submitted are not fraudulent.

■ Social Engineering and Pretexting

These are odd-sounding terms for potentially costly frauds. The definition for both refers to the act of deceiving people into divulging or providing access to confidential information that the perpetrator is not authorized to have, or into sending money in payment for purportedly legitimate goods, services, or—as in the high-profile case of Bernard Madoff—selling fraudulent financial investments. (Social engineering is also a form of confidence scheme like the one that was used in the first part of the Phoner Toner scam on page 97.) These schemes most often are committed in one of the following ways:

- **Telephone or in-person attempts** by a dishonest vendor, client, customer, or ex-employee to fraudulently obtain confidential information or unauthorized access to secure computer networks or databases that store confidential information. Such information may be employee identification numbers, credit card numbers, personal identification numbers, and other data that can be used to commit identity fraud.*

---

*It is important to remember that identity fraud is not the same as identity theft. The latter is the crime of fraudulently obtaining a person's confidential identifying information through social engineering as described above or by stealing the information. Identity fraud by contrast is the act of abusing this stolen information to fraudulently transact personal business in the victim's name. Identity frauds occur when the perpetrator poses as the victim to apply for credit cards, open bank accounts, make fraudulent on-line purchases, or fraudulently apply for personal loans or mortgages.

In these schemes, the perpetrator calls or approaches an employee, posing as someone he is not and provides a false but convincing reason why the employee should divulge confidential information such as the password or other access codes to a secure computer system that the caller is simply not authorized to have.

For example, an outsider may call your organization's human resources department, identifying herself as the administrative assistant of a senior executive and claiming that her boss has asked her to obtain the Social Security number, date of birth, and any other information on file for a particular manager who works for the executive. She may falsely state that the information is needed to verify facts about the manager's experience and background that her boss thinks are suspicious. Thinking nothing of this, the HR person happily provides this information, which is then used by the pretexter to commit identity crimes.

These crimes not only hurt the individual victims, but they also can do serious harm to your organization's reputation. A large company, for example, which loses substantial numbers of personal identifying records of employees, customers, vendors, and so on most likely will become the subject of news reports and perhaps even regulatory or law enforcement investigation. This can cause grave harm to the organization's image, making it difficult to meet sales goals, hire qualified people, and achieve its operational objectives.

Worse, a serious breach of your organization's confidential information security can result in enormous financial losses. Personal identifying information (PII) such as Social Security numbers, and health insurance and driver's license data must be fully secured in accordance with numerous state and federal laws and regulations. In addition, nearly every state now requires companies to notify individuals when their personal information has been lost, regardless of whether it was accidentally disclosed or was stolen during a cyber attack by computer or Internet criminals.

The problem is that notification alone is costly and, if not executed properly, may lead to litigation and government investigations. A recent study indicates, for example, that when an organization loses PII of customers, employees or others, each set of PII costs the victim organization nearly $200 in lost business, public relations, and legal expenses.[1]

■ **Web-based, e-mail, or phishing attacks.** You have no doubt received e-mail messages that appear to have been sent from your bank, Internet service provider, or credit card company urging you to click on a link to "update your account information." When these mass e-mails are sent out by Internet criminals, the links they want recipients to click on are actually phony Web pages that look like those of your actual bank, Internet service provider, or credit card company.

When victims fill in their credit card information and other personal data, it is actually automatically collected by the criminals who then use it to commit identity frauds like those described above. The next section of this chapter contains a graphic illustration of some of the red flags of this type of e-mail attack.

◀ **Case Study #14**

The Phoner Toner Scam

This crime usually involves a series of phone calls. In the first set of calls, the fraudster tries to find a new employee, temporary worker, or person who will freely give information. Posing as the organization's vendor, the caller asks the employee to read the make and model number of the nearest computer, printer, or photocopy machine. Faced with such a harmless-seeming request—and not realizing that a legitimate vendor would probably know the information already—the employee complies.

The problem comes in stage two of the ploy. Again posing as a vendor, the fraudster contacts someone at your office. If it is the same employee, he may be reminded of the earlier conversation as if the fraudster was an old friend. The employee hears about a tempting offer on toner cartridges that just happen to fit the organization's printer or copier.

Of course, there is a limited supply, or a limited time to order, so the employee is pressured to order a case or two. The caller may claim that his company is already an approved vendor and just needs a verbal agreement to authorize the sale.

Within a week or two, your organization receives invoices for toner "products" that were simply never legitimately ordered or received.*

How could this fraud have been prevented? List as many controls as you can. Compare yours with those listed in Appendix B.

1. _____

2. _____

3. _____

*Gregory Harris, Harris Consulting Group, writing at Tech Republic, www.techrepublic
.com.

Phishing is not only directed at an organization's customers or clients, or its confidential information. As Case Study #15 ("The Frito Fraud") shows, large corporations can also fall victim to well-orchestrated phishing e-mail attacks.

■ Bank Employee Collusion with Outsiders

If a bank branch manager, teller, or other employee with access to cash or bank checks wants to commit fraud, there are plenty of ways to do it. Often these crimes involve conspiracy with outside criminals. For example:

Jude Celestin and Ducarmel Edouard were convicted of bank fraud related to their roles in a counterfeit check cashing ring whose members stole almost $1 million.

Details. Celestin was an employee of Fleet Bank/Bank of America and provided the ring with business customer account information in order to create the counterfeit checks.

◀ Case Study #15

The Frito Fraud

Supervalu Inc., of Eden Prairie, Minnesota—a $40 billion grocery store chain—claimed in court that it received two separate e-mails, one purporting to be from an employee at Frito-Lay, Inc. and the second from American Greetings Corp. Both were Supervalu-approved vendors at the time. According to court documents, both e-mails instructed Supervalu to send future payments for each vendor to new bank accounts. For American Greetings, payments were to be wired to an HSBC bank account in Miami, Florida. For Frito-Lay, payments were to be sent to First Security Bank in Rogers, Arkansas.

In complying with the e-mails, Supervalu reportedly made numerous wire transfers totaling more than $6.5 million to the HSBC account and a total of $3.6 million to the account it was duped into believing belonged to Frito-Lay.

Following the discovery of the fraud, Supervalu notified the FBI, which was able to recover most of the money before it could be withdrawn from the accounts by the fraudsters.*

How could this fraud have been prevented? List as many controls as you can. Compare yours with those listed in Appendix B.

1. _____

2. _____

3. _____

*Documents in the cases of *United States v. The Sum of $3,597,929.68, More or Less,* 1:2007cv00165 (Dist. Idaho 2007) and *United States v. The Sum of $7,038,941.92, More or Less,* 1:2007cv00164 (Dist. Idaho 2007).

At trial, bank computer records showed Celestin searching for and accessing accounts of small businesses that were subsequently defrauded by the cashing of counterfeit checks. Edouard was a runner who cashed the counterfeit checks throughout Massachusetts.

Warning. These frauds are increasingly being orchestrated by organized crime rings. They will actually have their own operatives apply for jobs inside banks—as tellers or assistant branch managers. Once they are hired and have obtained access to confidential customer account data, they feed the information to their co-conspirators who then forge checks or credit cards and proceed to deplete the customer's accounts.

■ Customer-Perpetrated Fraud

Customers—either in the retail *or* commercial sector—can sometimes be just as deceptive as professional con artists. For retail companies, however, customer-perpetrated fraud is generally more serious and costly than it is for business-to-business organizations.

Phony returns of consumer merchandise are high on the list of customer frauds threatening retailers. According to the National Retail Federation (NRF), this type of fraud costs American retailers approximately $12 billion per year.[2] The most common fraudulent return ploys include:

- Returning stolen merchandise, with or without a receipt
- Returning merchandise with counterfeit receipts
- Returning merchandise bought with stolen or counterfeit credit cards or checks
- Organized Retail Fraud—mob or gang-initiated theft of large quantities of goods followed by mass production of forged receipts.

Another sobering statistic. E-Commerce fraud costs businesses $4 billion per year, according to CyberSource.[3] How it works:

- Online purchases are made with stolen or counterfeit credit cards.
- Fraudulent refunds: An e-commerce customer calls the merchant a week after placing an online order and claims not to have received the order.
- Fraudulent returns: The customer claims that substandard quality, service, or merchandise was delivered. This very often occurs when the product is already consumed and cannot be returned.

For example, former President George W. Bush's top domestic policy adviser Claude Allen—a protégé of Justice Clarence Thomas—admitted to "committing fraudulent returns" when a Target store manager confronted him as he was leaving with merchandise he had not paid for.

Allen's MO was as follows. He would purchase items, take them to his car, return to the store with the receipt, put identical items in a shopping bag and go to the customer service desk for refunds to his credit card.

■ Theft of Confidential Information

When committed by outsiders, these crimes are similar to social engineering and phishing in that they often have the same objective: to obtain confidential data about individuals—customers, clients, employees, or vendors—that can be used to commit the kinds of identity fraud described above.

However, when we refer to theft of confidential information in this context, we are referring to cyber attacks by outside computer criminals who know how to hack into your organization's secure computer systems and steal large amounts of protected information. It is often difficult to detect these attacks until after they have occurred and your customers, employers, vendors, or other related parties start becoming victims of identity fraud. However, the red flags of external fraud described in this chapter are tell-tale signs that external theft of confidential information could be occurring and can be stopped before it is too late.

Caution. In some instances outside information thieves steal large amounts of confidential data in order to extort the organization. They hack into secure computer systems or databases, steal the data, and then send an e-mail to the organization's top management with a sample of the data to prove it has been stolen along with the threat to post all of the stolen data on the Internet if the organization does not pay them what they demand. This is often referred to as "cyber extortion."

Another increasingly common way that outsiders steal confidential employee or other sensitive data is by stealing an organization's laptops. People who travel frequently on business must be extra careful never to leave a laptop unattended for just a moment—at an airport, a restaurant, or hotel. If a laptop does get stolen and the machine is not encrypted, the thief has immediate access to any information stored on the hard drive and may be able to sell it or use it to commit identity fraud.

For more information about cyber fraud, please refer to Appendix C.

Remember

The main difference between external fraudsters who steal information through social engineering and those who do it by phishing is that social engineers usually operate in person or over the phone, while phishing attackers use e-mail to commit their frauds. Laptop theft, however, is a crime involving *physical* theft of proprietary information.

▶ The "SCAM" Model

Every fraud involves at least one of four essential elements. To help you remember those that apply to external fraud, you can use the "SCAM Model." It is a retention tool to help you recognize the various types of external fraud that can affect your organization.

The SCAM Model:

S̲tealing is an external crime, but it is not a fraud unless something is stolen through such actions as deception, forgery, or counterfeiting. Usually it is money that can be stolen by forging checks, creating phony vendors, or collusion with insiders.

C̲onning comes from the word "confidence." The important part of conning is using persuasive language and behavior to make others believe things that are flat-out lies. Many conning cases are similar to the social engineering or pretexting schemes described earlier—where a fraudster poses as someone he is not and convinces the victim to give out information or even money, as in the case of Supervalu, Inc.

You have no doubt heard the term "con game." These are ploys where, as in the Phoner Toner scam, an outsider posing as a legitimate vendor convinces an employee to place an order and then sends an invoice expecting to get paid, even though the scammer has no intention of ever delivering anything.

A̲ltering is used in many external frauds involving business documents or checks. In check fraud, for example, a criminal may alter the payee or the amount of the check. This, along with numerous other altering ploys can be accomplished by simply erasing the existing print on the check and replacing it with fraudulent words or numbers, or by adding digits to make the check appear to be for more than it was originally made out for.

<u>M</u>isrepresenting. Does a vendor's name sound strange? It could mean that someone is posing as a vendor by sending an invoice with a phony address and is really just trying to steal from your organization.

Remember

The SCAM Model can be a valuable tool for helping to detect when a particular type of external fraud is occurring so that you can prevent it or report it to someone who can investigate and put a stop to such crimes.

▶ **Red Flags of External Fraud**

Now that you have a basic understanding of the main kinds of external fraud that can hurt an organization, it is time to move on to learn the red flags of these kinds of crimes.

Key. A solid familiarity with these tell-tale indicators of major forms of external fraud enables you to blow the whistle on fraudsters before they can cause major damage. For auditors or other financial professionals, many of these red flags point to potential fraud in an organization's financial reports and records.

To help remember the many red flags of external fraud, we have broken them down into the same categories that were used in the previous section.

Red Flags of Vendor and Billing Fraud

- Invoices appear unprofessionally prepared or printed.
- An employee receives unusual phone inquiries about office equipment or supplies.
- Key invoice information is missing, such as phone number, Employer Identification Number (EIN), and so forth.
- Suspicious invoice numbers: Two invoices received from the same company, one month apart, should *not* be numbered consecutively.
- A vendor name on an invoice does not show up on your Vendor Master Fraud or approved vendor list.
- The delivery address on the invoice differs from that of an approved vendor.
- Invoices are unfolded. This could indicate that an employee inserted a fraudulent invoice printed from his PC into a stack of legitimate invoices to be paid.
- Unusually high or low prices. This may indicate collusion between a vendor and purchasing employee.

- Unusual number of change orders. This is a potential sign of contractor billing fraud.
- A vendor's address matches that of an employee.

Red Flags of Social Engineering/Pretexting: In-Person or Telephone Attempts

- The caller sounds nervous or hesitant when making a request for information.
- The caller is unable to provide an adequate reason for needing the requested information.
- The caller's voice sounds familiar (could be an ex-employee or manager seeking unauthorized information).
- The caller's purported affiliation sounds suspicious ("Big Computer Services" or "LK Suppliers and Maintenance").

Red Flags of Bank Employee Collusion with Outsiders

- An unusually high volume of organization checks or debit transactions are found in a bank statement.
- An unusual number of cancelled checks appear to be forged.
- The account balance is suddenly declining at an unusual rate, with questionable transactions.

Red Flags of E-mail Phishing Attempts

- You receive unsolicited e-mail messages that ask, either directly or through a Website, for personal financial or identity information, such as bank account information, passwords, or other personal identifying information.
- An unsolicited e-mail message leads you to a supposedly secure Website that lacks the familiar "lock" icon at the bottom of your browser and "https" in front of the Website address.
- The e-mail message leads you to a Web page with an unusually long header address. Most legitimate sites have a relatively short Internet address that depicts the business name followed by ".com," or ".org." Spoofed sites often have exceedingly long strings of characters in the header, with the legitimate business name somewhere in the string, or not at all. Exhibit 5.2 shows a sample of a phishing e-mail message with the tell-tale signs of fraud circled.

Red Flags of Customer-Perpetrated Fraud

- A customer's credit card presented for a credit for a returned item appears counterfeit, and the customer claims not to have identification.
- Merchandise being frequently returned is identical to items that have recently been stolen from your store or other chain units.
- A receipt presented for a return appears counterfeit or forged (with unusual print or with a general appearance unlike normal receipts).
- Unusually high shrinkage rate (may indicate organized retail crime occurring).

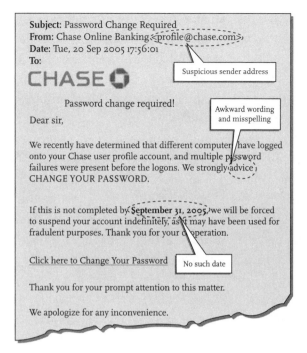

Exhibit 5.2 Example of a Phishing E-mail

Red Flags of Confidential Information Theft through Hacking

- Your IT Department detects a pattern of unauthorized attempts by outsiders to access a secure computer system.

- Employees, customers, vendors, or other individuals affiliated with your organization whose personal information is stored on systems call to ask about fraudulent use of their ID information.

- Employees, customers, or other affiliated individuals begin experiencing identity theft or fraud at the same time.

▶ Preventing External Fraud

Being able to recognize the red flags of fraud is the key to preventing and deterring it. When you know what kinds of fraud can occur at your organization and their tell-tale indicators, you have the knowledge necessary to put preventive procedures and controls in place to greatly reduce the organization's risk of being victimized by fraud.

Methods for minimizing the risk of external fraud in most organizations include:

- **Conducting a fraud risk assessment (FRA).** To successfully reduce your organization's vulnerability to fraud—either external or internal—you must first be able to categorize the specific types of fraud that *could* occur due to specific weaknesses in the organization's business operations and procedures.

    Note. Because more than one-half of all frauds are perpetrated by insiders, FRAs are best suited for detecting the risks of internal fraud. However, such assessments can also be valuable when the organization is especially vulnerable to different kinds of vendor schemes and other outsider scams, including attempts from foreign countries to hack into your organization's secure computer systems.

The first section of this chapter discussed the main types of external fraud. But that does not mean that all divisions or geographical locations of your organization are vulnerable to all of these frauds. So to prevent external fraud in the most efficient and cost-effective way, you must identify the areas in your organization's operations where specific types of external fraud could occur— and *how* they could be perpetrated. With that information, management can adjust its internal audit processes and train employees to screen for red flags of these specific types of fraud. If evidence of these frauds is discovered, it is then possible to design and implement internal controls to protect the organization against those specific fraud risks. This is precisely what an FRA is designed to do.

Chapter 6 demonstrates the essential steps for conducting an FRA. Suffice it for now to say that such an assessment will be helpful to the external fraud prevention effort, in terms of providing the necessary guidance for management to detect red flags of actual or potential fraud and to put into place well-designed internal controls that minimize the risks of all frauds that could threaten the organization.

- **Implement segregation of duties (SoD).** As discussed in Chapter 3, this term refers to separating job functions in a way that no single employee is in a position to circumvent controls against process-level internal fraud. SoD is equally important in the context of external fraud. Specifically, responsibilities should be separated in a way that prevents a single employee from being deceived by an external fraudster or from gaining sufficient authority to collude with a vendor, client, or ex-employee.

  Example of basic SoD. Never have the same person approving invoices and generating checks to vendors. A dishonest vendor could submit fraudulent invoices that deceive the person in charge of approvals and then get paid by the same individual.

  Better. Make one employee responsible for reviewing and approving invoices and *another* responsible for disbursements. That way, at least one of the people should catch any fraudulent billing that a dishonest vendor may be attempting. Similarly, authorization by two managers should be required for all expenditures exceeding a set maximum for single-manager approval.

- **Implement delegation of duties (DoA).** As defined on page 50 in Chapter 3, this term refers to establishing specific levels of authority indicating who is permitted to approve purchases and other business transactions, for what items, and for what amount. It is just as important in minimizing external fraud risk as it is in preventing internal fraud.

  Also important. Never allow a single purchasing staff member to approve the addition of a new vendor to the approved vendor list. Ideally, this should be done by a special committee representing different business functions and applying an agreed-upon set of standards or criteria for approving new vendors. Such standards should include, for example, length of time in business, record of customer/client complaints against the vendor, legal or regulatory actions against the vendor, and references from existing clients or customers.

- **Train employees who have direct contact with vendors.** For example, make them aware of the common scams and schemes that vendors use to steal from your organization; employees in the procurement, accounts payable, accounting, and contracting functions will be better able to prevent vendor fraud from occurring. The same applies to employees with direct customer contact.

- **Train employees who have direct contact with customers.** Demonstrate to all sales personnel and register operators the tell-tale signs of bogus credit cards and receipts, and stolen merchandise.

- **Regularly review your approved vendor list(s).** If a dishonest vendor has somehow managed to slip through the new-vendor approval process and is committing fraud by submitting phony or duplicate invoices or by overcharging your organization, a semiannual review of the approved vendor list will spot this and prevent further abuse.

- **Train all employees in essential information security policies.** The organization has put essential data security technologies into place to protect the organization against outside hackers trying to steal confidential financial, employee, or customer data or so-called malicious code attacks (generally a fancy term for viruses).

  However, it is critical that everyone who uses a computer that is linked to an in-house network and/or to the Internet exercise security-conscious computing practices. For example:

  - Never leave passwords written on paper in plain sight.
  - Always turn your computer off when not using it.
  - Use caution when shopping online, using instant messaging, or wireless services to reduce your risk of identity theft. (Make sure the site address starts with https://.)
  - Install a firewall and up-to-date antivirus software.
  - Regularly back up your data on an external hard drive or a removable storage device.
  - Never click on links in e-mail messages that are in any way suspicious—especially if they ask you to update your account information.

▶ Review Points

- External fraud, though less costly than internal fraud, is still a major threat to most organizations.
- Social engineering schemes—including telephone, in-person, and electronic/phishing schemes prey on people's tendency to trust others.

- These schemes, which usually are motivated by the intention to commit identity fraud, not only hurt the ID fraud victims, but the organization as well. When customers, employees, and vendors fear that their confidential information is not secure, they may go to a competitor.

- The SCAM Model—defining Stealing, Conning, Altering, and Misrepresenting—can be a valuable tool for detecting when a particular type of external fraud is occurring, so you can prevent it or report it to someone who can investigate and put a stop to such crimes.

- Vendor/billing fraud includes such schemes as double billing, creating phony vendors, and delivering substandard products or services at full price.

- The essentials of detecting the red flags and preventing external fraud include performing a fraud risk assessment (FRA), training employees with direct contact with vendors and customers, segregation of duties (SoD), and regular review of your approved vendor list.

▶ Chapter Quiz

True or False:

Using the SCAM Model, (**S**tealing, **C**onning, **A**ltering, and **M**isrepresenting), choose the correct answer:

1. A delivery address on an invoice of an approved vendor that differs from the one on the approved vendor list is an example of both **S**tealing and **M**isrepresenting.
   - ❏ True   ❏ False

2. A job applicant with a very impressive resume gets hired to work as a supervisor. Six months later, he gets caught submitting excessive expense reports, asking for reimbursement of expenses for which he has no receipts. This is an example of **A**ltering.
   - ❏ True   ❏ False

3. The Phoner Toner scam in which an outside fraudster attempts to convince an employee that he is the company's approved office supply vendor is an example of **S**tealing, **C**onning, and **M**isrepresenting.
   - ❏ True   ❏ False

Circle the correct answer to the following questions:

4. Which of the following is *not* a type of external fraud?
   - **a.** Delivery of substandard goods at full price
   - **b.** Creating phony vendors

    c. Phishing attacks

    d. Cheating on travel expense reports

5. Circle *all* of the choices that represent a red flag of vendor/supplier fraud:

    a. Invoices appear unprofessionally prepared.

    b. Consecutive invoice numbers within a one-month period.

    c. Invoices are properly folded.

    d. Delivery address on an invoice differs from that of an approved vendor.

6. Circle the choice that is *not* an essential preventive measure against external fraud:

    a. Fraud risk assessment

    b. Educating all employees with direct contact with vendors

    c. Conducting background checks on all new employees

    d. Segregation of duties

Fill in the blank:

7. One of the common ways that fraudsters obtain confidential information is by social _____.

8. Phishing attackers use _____ to commit their crimes.

9. A vendor's name that seems strange could be a red flag of the SCAM model's element of _____.

10. An essential step in preventing billing schemes is to regularly review the approved _____ list.

For the answers, please turn to Appendix A.

CHAPTER SIX

Conducting a Successful Fraud Risk Assessment

Over the past several years, much has been made among anti-fraud professionals of so-called fraud risk assessments (FRA). These are analyses of an organization's *risks of being victimized by specific types of fraud* and are typically conducted by its external auditors. Increasingly, however, *internal* auditors are being pressured by senior management to conduct FRAs of their own. This often is prudent because internal auditors know better than outside auditors how the organization's financial and business operations function and can therefore more readily understand how fraud could occur in particular processes, transactions, and business procedures.

Some anti-fraud experts claim that having internal auditors conduct FRAs is unwise since these individuals are on the organization's payroll and therefore lack the independence required to objectively analyze weaknesses that could provide opportunities for fraudsters. However, the same can be said for external auditors. While not employees of the organization, they are paid by their clients to conduct FRAs, thus establishing the same potential compromise of independence.

The bottom line. The Institute of Internal Auditors has endorsed audit standards that outline the techniques and procedures for conducting an FRA—specifically those contained in *Statement of Auditing Standards #99 (SAS 99)*. In this (and other) key guidelines, an FRA is meant to guide auditors and fraud examiners in adjusting their audit plans and testing to focus on gathering evidence of potential fraud schemes and scenarios identified by the FRA. In essence, responding to the FRA's findings requires the auditor to adjust the timing, nature, and extent of testing, in such ways as:

- Performing procedures at physical locations on a surprise or unannounced basis by, for example, observing inventory on unexpected dates or at unexpected locations or counting cash on a surprise basis.

- Requesting that inventories be counted at the end of the reporting period or on a date closer to period-end to minimize the risk of manipulation of balances in the period between the date of completion of the count and the end of the reporting period.

- Making oral inquiries of major customers and vendors in addition to sending written confirmations, or sending confirmation requests to a specific party within an organization.

- Performing substantive analytical procedures using disaggregated data by, for example, comparing gross profit or operating margins by location, type of service, line of business, or month to auditor-developed expectations.

- Interviewing personnel involved in activities in areas where a risk of material misstatement due to fraud has been identified (such as at the country or regional level) to obtain their insights about the risk and how controls could address the risk.[1]

Lesson for all. It is essential that most internal financial managers and audit professionals understand how to conduct an FRA, in order to thoroughly assess the organization's exposure to specific frauds so that they can perform the kind of direct role described above. That role must lead to management's formulation and implementation of the *specific,* customized controls referred to in the preceding three chapters. These are the measures that go *beyond* the basic, *essential* controls outlined in those chapters; they optimize the organization's defenses against these risks. As such, they vary from organization to organization, in accordance with the particular processes and procedures that may be vulnerable to fraud.

For example, Company A may process invoices in such a tightly controlled way—with double or triple approvals of new vendors, manual review of all invoices, and so on—that an FRA reveals few if any areas where red flags of vendor fraud can be found. Company B by contrast may process invoices by simply having the appropriate department head review and approve them. In that case, an FRA would raise red flags of potential fraud that could occur through double billing, sham company schemes, or collusion.

Critical. As *SAS 99* indicates,

> Some risks are inherent in the environment of the entity, but most can be addressed with an appropriate system of internal control.
>
> Once fraud risk assessment has taken place, the entity can identify the processes, controls, and other procedures that are needed to mitigate the identified risks. Effective internal controls will include well-developed control environment, an effective and secure information system, and appropriate control and monitoring activities.
>
> Because of the importance of information technology in supporting operations and the processing of transactions, management also needs to implement and maintain appropriate controls, whether automated or manual, over computer-generated information.[2]

The FRA provides the roadmap for management to determine where existing controls need tightening and where nonexistent controls must be formulated, implemented, and monitored for effectiveness.

As you'll learn in Chapter 8 of this workbook, the FRA's findings will show auditors where they must adjust their audit approach to screen specifically for red flags of fraud risks—and then to discuss with management how to strengthen controls against them.

> The heart of an effective internal controls systems and the effectiveness of an anti-fraud program are . . . contingent on an effective risk management assessment.
> —**Dr. Tommie Singleton, CPA, University of Alabama**

Knowing where and how specific frauds could occur in the organization will guide investigators and auditors in detecting the red flags of potential wrongdoing. The FRA is the best technique for accomplishing this.

Important. Although conducting an FRA is not terribly difficult, it does require careful planning and methodical execution. The structure and culture of the organization dictates how the FRA is formulated. In general, however, there is a mainstream form of FRA that the audit and fraud prevention communities have agreed on. The following pages outline the essentials of that approach.

As the AICPA, IIA, and ACFE's *Managing the Business Risk of Fraud* points out, "Assessing the likelihood and significance of each potential fraud risk is a subjective process that should consider not only monetary significance, but also significance to an organization's reputation and its legal and regulatory compliance requirements. An initial assessment of fraud risk should consider the inherent risk of a particular fraud in the absence of any known controls that may address the risk. An organization can cost-effectively manage its fraud risks by assessing the likelihood and significance of fraudulent behavior."[3]

Key. While your FRA must be tailored to your organization's specific business functions, structure, and culture, there are several basic FRA methods that apply to most conventional FRAs.

■ Step 1: Create an FRA Team

The FRA team leaders should include a senior internal auditor (or the Chief Internal Auditor if feasible) and/or an experienced outside certified fraud examiner with substantial experience in conducting FRAs for organizations in your business or nonprofit sector.

Other members of the team should include:

- CFO
- Head of purchasing or procurement
- Senior internal audit manager
- Senior risk management manager
- Senior HR manager
- External consultant(s) with expertise in fraud detection and prevention

■ Step 2: Identify the Organization's Universe of Potential Risks

Your starting point is to determine what fraud schemes and scenarios typically affect organizations in your industry in general—and in your organization in particular. Next, you must assess the potential for these schemes and scenarios existing in your organization, based on the culture of the organization and on its current framework of internal controls.

Details. Employee fraud and embezzlement are most likely to occur in organizations with especially poor tone at the top, weak internal controls and poor accounting practices. It is also widely accepted that organizations with a culture of excessive emphasis on financial performance—at the expense of employee morale, team spirit, and high-quality work results—are likeliest to be targeted by internal fraudsters.

Key. To identify your organization's specific risks of fraud, the FRA calls for the team leader to conduct brainstorming sessions with the team to develop a listing from what is referred to in *Managing the Business Risk of Fraud* as the "population" of fraud schemes and scenarios likeliest to occur in the organization.[4] This is often done by evaluating an existing list of common frauds, such as the more than 150 generic fraud schemes developed by PricewaterhouseCoopers Fraud Risk and Controls Practice Leader, Jonny Frank. Frank broke down this large body of fraud schemes into six key categories:

- Fraudulent financial reporting
- Misappropriation of assets
- Expenditures and liabilities for an improper purpose
- Revenue and assets obtained by fraud
- Costs and expenses avoided by fraud
- Financial misconduct by senior management.[5]

Important. To help in this exercise—and to add specific fraud schemes and scenarios to the results of brainstorming sessions—you should focus on each key business process in which particular types of fraud from these categories *could* occur, such as improper revenue recognition (fraudulent financial reporting), theft and forgery of organization checks (misappropriation of assets), paying bribes (expenditures for an improper purpose), misrepresentation of the value of assets for sale (revenue obtained by fraud), nonpayment of taxes (costs avoided by fraud), and round-tripping transactions (financial misconduct by senior management).

In each area, obtain detailed answers to the following questions from managers, supervisors, and/or line employees in each function:

- What types of fraud have occurred or been suspected in the past?
- What types of fraud could be committed against the organization?
- What are the specific ways that employees or managers could commit fraud by acting alone?
- What specific ways could vendors commit fraud in your area?
- How could vendors working in collusion with your co-workers commit fraud?

■ Step 3: Analyze the Likelihood of Each Scheme or Scenario Occurring

Fraud risk assessments (FRAs) must consider the likelihood that a particular fraud will occur. International auditing standards specify the following risk levels:

- Remote
- More than Remote
- Reasonably Possible
- Probable

■ Step 4: Assess the Materiality of Risk

In this step, according to Frank, you must identify fraud risks that could have an important financial impact on the organization, according to a shareholder, lender, or other user of the organization's financial reports.[6] There are three main categories of materiality:

1. Inconsequential
2. More than Inconsequential
3. Material

As discussed in Chapter 8, any risks that are more than inconsequential must be addressed by auditors to gather detailed evidence of potential fraudulent activity.

■ Step 5: Assess Risks within the Context of Existing Anti-Fraud Controls

Your FRA team should identify the control activities for those fraud risks that have a more-than-remote likelihood of occurring and that could result in a substantial (or "material" in audit/accounting terminology) loss to the organization. This is because once the FRA and subsequent fraud-auditing work is done, you will know exactly what controls are missing or require strengthening.

Another way to get to the same result is by evaluating the effectiveness of existing controls in preventing specific fraud scenarios. This process aims to assign a numerical grade for the likelihood of a specific fraud scheme occurring with the existing control in place.

How it works. Assess specific controls in place for preventing occurrence of the various fraud scenarios. This enables auditors to determine how likely (or unlikely) it is—on a scale of one to three—that such a scenario will actually occur based on the controls in place, with "One" representing the most effective possible risk mitigation. For example:

One. Control design optimally minimizes the occurrence of the fraud risk *and minimizes control failures.*

Two. Control design *reasonably* minimizes the occurrence of the fraud risk.

Three. Control design *does not* minimize the occurrence of the fraud risk.[7]

The bottom line. The ultimate objective of any FRA is to provide guidance to your auditors in adjusting their audit plans to incorporate specific audit techniques for detecting fraud and to assist management in formulating and/or adjusting its anti-fraud controls to reduce the risk of fraud.

Chapter 7 describes *general* fraud detection measures that most organizations must put into place, but which do *not* involve audit practices. With that background, however, Chapter 8 *will* provide you with a description of several of the specific audit procedures designed to detect frauds whose risk has been identified through conducting your FRA.

Remember

In effective FRAs, the FRA team and your internal audit department must consider whether and how anti-fraud controls can be circumvented or overridden by management and others. They should also analyze both internal and external threats to confidential electronic data, and computer and network security.

▶ The Roles of the Board and Management in Fraud Risk Assessments[8]

None of the steps outlined above for conducting an FRA will occur, let alone be effectively conducted, without direct guidance and buy-in from top management and the board. The board of directors has the responsibility to ensure that management designs effective fraud-risk management procedures. Generally, the board delegates this oversight responsibility to the audit committee.

Important. The board should detail these responsibilities in the audit committee's charter as well as its own. That way, there is minimal opportunity for passing the buck by board or audit committee members who may feel that doing an FRA is either too costly or not worthwhile.

To ensure that appropriate steps are taken to identify and prioritize the fraud risks for your organization, the audit committee should:

- **Ensure that management assigns the responsibility of FRA and management of identified risks to a qualified individual.** Though many individuals within the organization must be *involved* in the FRA, many organizations undermine their FRA processes by failing to put someone in charge of coordinating the process and reporting to the audit committee. Often, a senior member of the organization's internal audit (IA) department is best qualified to take on this role. In other organizations, the chief financial officer is best equipped to do it.

  The key is to determine which senior manager has the experience, training, and staff resources to conduct your FRA and to then make that person fully accountable for conducting and reporting on the FRA by specified deadlines.

- **Evaluate the FRA process and methodology implemented by management.** The audit committee must understand and question management on the methods used to conduct an FRA. The aim is to constantly improve the effectiveness *and* efficiency of the FRA process.

  Aim. To ensure that the organization's fraud risks are properly prioritized by using an effective ranking system, as discussed above.

  Effective. Because there is no single standard for conducting an FRA, the methodology and documentation of the risk assessment process must be tailored to the organization's size, complexity, industry, and goals. Internal audit's familiarity with these factors again often proves valuable in determining whether management's risk assessment methodology is effective.

- **Be aware of and concur with management's risk tolerance.** It is impossible to address every fraud risk that is revealed by the risk assessment process. There are simply not enough financial and human resources to eliminate all of the vulnerabilities that exist at any given time. Internal audit or whichever team is responsible for conducting and reporting on the FRA must therefore prioritize and report to management and the audit committee on its ranking of the fraud risk it has identified.

The audit committee must then monitor and be prepared to question management's choice to downgrade the threat of certain key fraud risks. For example, internal audit may determine through the FRA process that ACH fraud is not a serious threat to the organization because all of the available anti-fraud controls (for instance, debit blocks, debit filters, and account segregation) have been well established and are accomplishing the goal of minimizing the risk of this type of fraud.

It is the audit committee's job to ensure that it is getting up-to-date analyses such as this from internal audit and then to determine if it concurs with the analysis or not, and to press for better internal controls where it sees the need for them.

▶ Review Points

- A fraud risk assessment (FRA) is an analysis of an organization's *risks of being victimized by specific types of fraud.*

- Approaches to FRAs will differ from organization to organization, but most FRAs will focus on identifying fraud risks in six key categories: (1) fraudulent financial reporting, (2) misappropriation of assets, (3) expenditures and liabilities for an improper purpose, (4) revenue and assets obtained by fraud, (5) costs and expenses avoided by fraud, and (6) financial misconduct by senior management.

- A properly conducted FRA guides auditors in adjusting their audit plans and testing to focus specifically on gathering evidence of possible fraud.

- Being able to conduct an FRA is essential to effective assessment of the viability of existing anti-fraud controls and to strengthening the organization's inadequate controls, as identified by the results of your FRA.

- In addition to assessing the *types* of fraud for which your organization is at risk, the FRA assesses the *likelihood* that each of those frauds might occur.

- After the FRA and subsequent fraud-auditing work is completed, the FRA team should have a good idea of the specific controls needed to minimize the organization's vulnerability to fraud.

- Auditing for fraud is a critical next step after assessing fraud risks, and this requires auditing for evidence of frauds that may exist according to the red flags turned up by your FRA.

▶ Chapter Quiz

True or False:

1. Fraud risk assessments are typically conducted by an organization's external auditors—not its internal auditors.
   - ❏ True   ❏ False

2. FRAs often produce better results when internal auditors conduct them, instead of external auditors, because internal auditors are more familiar with the organization's internal workings.
   - ❏ True   ❏ False

3. The board of directors in most organizations delegates oversight of the FRA process to the governance committee.
   - ❏ True   ❏ False

4. An FRA is meant to guide executives in gathering evidence of potential fraud schemes and scenarios identified by the FRA.
   - ❏ True   ❏ False

Circle the correct answer to the following questions:

5. Which of the following is not a critical member of the FRA team?
   - a. Finance manager
   - b. Regional audit manager
   - c. Director of procurement
   - d. Information technology (IT) director

6. Which of the following is *not* a risk level of fraud that is assigned to specific fraud risks identified by an FRA?
   - a. Remote
   - b. Extremely likely

    c. More than remote

    d. Reasonably possible

Fill in the blank:

7. One of the key exercises in an FRA is determining the _____ of specific fraud schemes or scenarios occurring.

8. The ultimate objective of conducting an FRA is to optimize _____.

9. The appropriate exercise for identifying the organization's specific fraud risk is a _____ session.

10. The three generally accepted categories for ranking the materiality of a specific fraud risk are inconsequential, more than inconsequential, and _____.

For the answers, please turn to Appendix A.

Basic Fraud Detection Tools and Techniques

By now you have a good familiarity with the many types of fraud at both the employee level and the management level. You have also learned how to identify many of the red flags, basic anti-fraud controls, and risk assessment methods that must be in place as the foundation of an effective anti-fraud program.

Now it is time to dig a little deeper and learn how to ensure that the red flags of fraud (or potential fraud) *are not missed*—by internal financial managers *or* by employees throughout the organization.

Key. While fraud *prevention* is always more effective and less costly than fraud *detection* (and subsequent investigation), prevention is unfortunately not always possible. That is why mastering key detection techniques is essential for financial professionals. It is also why we spent considerable time in earlier chapters learning about the red flags of employee-level and management-level fraud and how to assess the risks of specific types of fraud for your organization.

Once internal auditors and financial managers know what to look for, there is a good chance that fraud or suspicious activity will be detected one way or another, *but only if the organization has the proper monitoring, reporting, and other detection procedures in place.*

Note. Some of the following fraud detection techniques may sound similar to certain anti-fraud controls discussed in Chapter 5. This is because there is often a fine line between detection and prevention. In fact, some detection steps *overlap* with prevention methods, as in the case of conflict of interest where enforcing a management financial disclosure policy may both detect conflicting financial interests *and* prevent frauds resulting from them by virtue of the actual detection of the relationships.

In general, however, such overlap does not exist, and carefully assessing the descriptions of prevention and detection methods clarifies that there is usually an important distinction between the two.

There are numerous procedures and techniques for detecting actual or potential fraud. In the interest of simplicity, we'll divide them into two segments: Basic and Advanced.

Basic detection techniques and procedures typically involve screening for operational fraud and involve manual, nonauditing measures.

By contrast, detailed detection is designed for catching frauds such as those whose red flags are found in the organization's financial records and statements. They depend heavily on specific anti-fraud auditing techniques designed to measure the organization's risks of fraud and then using professional skepticism and unique audit measures to detect evidence of these specific fraud risks.

This chapter addresses the basic detection tools and procedures that *all* employees in the organization should be familiar with. Chapter 8 addresses the advanced, audit-related techniques that must be used in direct response to the findings of your fraud risk assessment (FRA) in order to identify red flags of fraud in the organization's financial records and to collect supporting evidence of these potential frauds so that management can determine whether a full-fledged fraud investigation is warranted.

Remember

Internal auditors and financial managers are increasingly expected to detect fraud. However, it is *everyone's* responsibility to play a role in Preventing, Detecting, and Reporting Fraud.

▶ Basic Fraud Detection

It is generally agreed by the audit and accounting professions that internal and external auditors *are not* expected to be the organization's primary fraud detectives. However, in light of exploding fraud in both the operational and financial reporting areas throughout the economy, there is growing pressure for auditors—as well as internal financial managers—to develop and exercise effective fraud detection and screening skills and practices.

As PricewaterhouseCoopers points out in a major report on forensic accounting, "Internal auditors should improve their fraud detection skills and should program fraud detection into their work plans. Internal auditors should also be ready to exercise integrity and courage when the situation calls for it."[1]

The place to start is in the area of basic fraud detection in operational activities, such as embezzlement, collusion, cash and inventory theft, check fraud, and information theft.

Here are the important basic detection measures you should have in place at all times:

■ **Surprise audits.** When dishonest employees are aware of scheduled audits, it is easy for them to conceal their fraudulent activities. For example, unscrupulous auditors or managers can have workplace, warehouse, or plant tours prearranged to guide external auditors to areas where signs of inventory theft or manipulation (or other schemes) are not evident. Or they can conceal documentation that might lead the auditors to suspect misconduct.

Solution. Set up unannounced audits by external auditors or fraud examiners. Organizations that conduct these exercises once or twice a year and tell employees *only* that they can expect such an audit at any time not only are likely to detect fraud that is unconcealed when employees are caught off balance, but they also put a powerful anti-fraud *deterrent* into place. Employees who, though dishonest, are smart enough not to get caught, will be less likely to perpetrate financial crimes if they know that they may be investigated at any time.

- **Surveillance.** Installing closed-circuit television cameras, using mystery shoppers, confidential informants, and other surveillance techniques can be effective in detecting physical fraud such as theft of supplies or inventory, abuse of company equipment or other physical assets, and check interception in mailrooms and other areas where large volumes of incoming and outgoing checks are handled.

    Caution. Implementing these detection techniques requires planning and implementation by an experienced fraud examiner or investigator. If your organization does not employ such an individual, you can retain one of the many qualified independent fraud examiners. For help in locating one in your area, contact the Association of Certified Fraud Examiners at www.acfe.com.

- **Regular internal audits.** While, as mentioned earlier, auditors are not expected to be fraud prevention specialists, there is growing pressure on internal auditors to focus on the detection of illegal activity. Chapter 8 discusses how this can be achieved using specially-designed anti-fraud audit measures. However, as far as *basic* fraud detection is concerned, internal auditors should start by adopting a mindset of professional skepticism in determining the existence and seriousness of fraud risks in their regular internal audits. This is an intellectual approach to auditing that *assumes* that evidence of fraud exists in the organization's books and records, and that proper attention to the details of such documentation—within the context of existing internal controls against fraud—will inevitably result in discovery of evidence of such illegal activity.

    In fact, as PricewaterhouseCoopers states, "professional skepticism is a key attribute of an effective auditor."[2]

    According to *Statement of Auditing Standards (SAS) No. 99,* and similarly reflected in *International Standard of Auditing (ISA) #240* (both of which are discussed in detail in Chapter 8), professional skepticism calls for the auditor to "[t]horoughly probe the issues, acquire additional evidence as necessary, and consult with other team members and, if appropriate, experts in the [organization], rather than rationalize or dismiss information or other conditions that indicate [that] fraud may have occurred."[3]

    This approach will serve auditors well in the fraud detection process as they move on to conduct:

- **Ratio analysis of the organization's key financial records.** This involves quantifying the relationship between two different financial statement amounts.

Key. When anomalies are found from one accounting period to the next in any of the following basic financial ratios, there is reason to dig deeper for hard evidence of fraud:

- *Current ratio* (current assets compared with current liabilities.) A check fraud embezzlement scheme or other internal theft will usually create an unusual drop in the ratio.

- *Inventory turnover* (cost of goods sold compared with average inventory). If an employee is stealing inventory, that ratio will usually cause this ratio to jump, as missing inventory is written off and the resulting cost of goods sold increases.

    Example. When there are unusual spikes or dips in your organization's inventory ratio, this could be a sign that theft of supplies or other inventory is being perpetrated, or that a procurement or kickback scheme is in progress.

- *Debt-to-equity ratio* (total liabilities compared with total equity). If this ratio is increasing, along with a comparable increase in accounts payable, it may mean that fraudulent invoicing or other schemes are causing total liabilities to increase at an unusual rate.

- *Margin analysis* (sales minus cost of goods sold). If embezzlement or another form of internal fraud is in progress, it will usually increase the cost of goods sold, which in turn will reduce the margin to an unusual level.

- *Collection ratio* (days in a year divided by receivables turnover). Also known as days sales outstanding, this is often a good indicator of a possible fictitious sales scheme. If sales are increasing unusually rapidly, that will cause the ratio to increase, possibly indicating the existence of such a scheme.

- *Vertical analysis*, which involves assessment of patterns in specific accounts such as sales and expenses by reflecting each line item as a percentage of net sales, and comparing the relationships to those of other periods. If, for example, the former is increasing at an unusually rapid rate while the latter is declining, there is a possibility that some sort of book-cooking scheme is going on. Further audit-related investigation will be required.

- *Horizontal analysis*, which involves assessment of patterns in specific accounts, balance sheet or income statement accounts, and comparing the percentage changes to other periods: for example, placing the quarterly income statements side by side for a two- or three-year period, and evaluating the percentage changes of income and expense line items across the periods.[4]

- **Physical review of organization-owned supplies and asset inventory.** As mentioned earlier, if your organization's operational processes require use of large volumes of raw materials supplies, computer system hardware, and other physical assets, there is an ongoing temptation for employees with direct access to these products to steal them.

    Result. One of the most important basic fraud detection techniques that all divisions of your organization should implement is regular physical inventory checks—together with complete record keeping.

Caution. These records should never be kept by individuals with access to the assets being counted.

- **Manual review of T&E claims.** This is often challenging when an organization has many employees taking frequent business trips or making purchases on behalf of the organization. However, detecting fraud in T&E does *not* require manual review of every receipt or boarding pass. Random but frequent manual review of individual reimbursement claims is usually enough to detect specific incidents of fraud and to establish a strong deterrent for employees with travel and expenses privileges who might be tempted to fudge their expenses if the organization did *no* manual review of reimbursement claims.

- **Manual assessment of payroll information.** One highly effective way to detect payroll fraud—such as creation of ghost employees by payroll managers—is to do a periodic, unannounced manual distribution of paychecks, requiring all employees to show ID to receive their checks. Any unclaimed paychecks should be compared against the master payroll file. If unclaimed checks have addresses matching those of legitimate employees, chances are the legitimate employees are perpetrating a ghost employee scheme.

  Also effective. Look for cashed paychecks with dual endorsements. This may be evidence of a legitimate payroll manager colluding with a live ghost who is endorsing the paycheck over to the employee who also endorses it before cashing or depositing it.

  Important. Be suspicious of any employee who takes no holiday or sick leave. A ghost employee would obviously take neither—unless the payroll or human resources manager is perpetrating the fraud and creates fictitious records of the ghost's time off.

- **Manual review of all vendors.** As you learned, there are countless varieties of vendor or billing schemes that fraudsters try to perpetrate against organizations whose anti-fraud controls are weak. Detecting these crimes can be challenging. And while special anti-fraud audit techniques can often do the trick (see Chapter 8), there are important basic detection methods to follow on a regular basis. For example:

  - Look for situations where payments to a vendor substantially exceed the budgeted amount—especially when the disbursed amount is exactly double the budgeted amount. This is a sign of possible double-billing by either a phony vendor or by a dishonest legitimate vendor who receives the first check, while a dishonest conspirator in the accounts payable department takes the second.

  - Periodically (at least twice a year) examine details and patterns in the organization's largest accounts. Those are typically where fraudsters attempt to hide their billing schemes—hoping that the stolen amounts will not raise any red flags in large-dollar accounts.

  - Regularly test to confirm that vendors are legitimate. You do not have to investigate every vendor in every business unit—just those added since the last audit. To confirm their legitimacy, call them up and interview them, or search for them on the Internet, or check local or national business data-bases for licenses, or contact others who have used them.

- Print out your business unit's entire vendor list alphabetically and examine any two (or more) vendors with the same or similar addresses.

- **Have all bank reconciliations conducted by a manager outside of the accounts payable or procurement area.** Screen for fraudulently signed or endorsed checks, checks for suspicious amounts, to suspicious payees, and so on.

Important note. When it comes to basic detection techniques for computer or electronic data–related frauds, remember that it is extremely difficult to proactively detect these crimes before they occur. That is because most of them are committed by computer-savvy employees who are able to access secure databases without detection. The best detection method is to have a trained IT employee regularly screen for unusual employee requests for access to secure databases and for unusual attempts to access secure systems, and to manually monitor computer and network activity for signs of suspicious activity.

- **Confidential fraud hotline**

Details. A confidential (and anonymous) fraud hotline gives employees at all levels a way to report to management indicators of embezzlement, kickbacks, collusion, and other operational frauds without fear of retribution or retaliation. As such it is one of the most important basic fraud detection tools any organization can have.

Important. Research has shown that employees who have a confidential hotline at their disposal and who are trained in the red flags of fraud are likely to report such red flags when they identify them. In fact, as discussed earlier, employee tips represent the most common way that fraud is detected. While hotlines are not the *only* mechanism used to communicate those tips (direct contact with a supervisor is preferred by many whistle-blowers), they certainly play a critical role in enabling employees who detect signs of fraud to come forward and report them.

Further supporting the argument in favor of implementing a hotline is the fact that doing so is quite inexpensive. Even if you use a third-party independent hotline service, the cost is insignificant compared to the cost of fraud that would otherwise go unreported.

Making it work. A hotline is only as effective as the people who run it. The most productive hotline systems are those operated by outside vendors whose employees are trained in how to field calls from employees, vendors, donors, and others. They know how to filter out inevitable frivolous calls—and how to converse with legitimate whistle-blowers in order to obtain as much evidence of fraud as possible to enable management to decide how to pursue each case.

Martin Biegelman, director of the Financial Integrity Unit at Microsoft Corp. and Joel Bartow, director of Fraud Prevention at ClientLogic addressed the common problem of employee reluctance to blow the whistle:

"Because whistle-blowers are often reluctant and nervous about making hot-line calls, the operators who answer these calls must be extremely careful to avoid causing undue anxiety or stress that might cause the caller to get 'cold feet' and abruptly end the call."[5]

Key. They must be skilled in coaxing answers from callers without intimidating them. From the very first moments of the call they must convey an encouraging and supportive tone, respect for the caller, and patience in understanding what the caller is trying to communicate. *Specific guidelines for handling whistleblower calls include:*

- **Assure the caller that the call is confidential** and advise him that there is no obligation to be identified at any time unless the caller specifically asks to be identified.

- **Record the time and date of the call.**

- **Record the operator's name, identification number, and location.**

- **Assign a caller ID code or number.**

- **Ask if the caller is an employee, vendor, contractor, customer, or other.**

- **Ask for as many details as the caller can provide regarding the specific fraud incident.** Try to find out how the caller became aware of the incident.

- **Ask which individuals are involved in the incident,** including names, titles, addresses, and any other contact information the caller may have.

- **Find out when the incident occurred** and if it is still ongoing.

- **Ask for any physical or electronic evidence** that the caller may have that is directly related to the incident.

- **Inform the caller that while she may have the opportunity to provide additional information at a later date, it is advisable to share as much detail as possible now** to enable the organization to effectively follow up on the call.[6]

For additional detailed information on how to establish and manage a hotline, download Deloitte's very useful report, *2006 Corporate Governance and Compliance Hotline Benchmarking Report* at www.tnwinc.com/downloads/2006 BenchmarkingReport.pdf.

◀ Case Study #16

I'm the Boss, and I Can Use Any Vendors I Want

As a top executive of a large company, Sherman Sham had authority to approve vendor invoices and have them processed for payment by the company's accounts payable department. To facilitate payment of bogus invoices, Sherman also submitted fraudulent vendor forms in the names of three friends or bogus companies controlled by them. Checks issued by the company in payment of the invoices went to Sherman's friends who had set up bank accounts. A total of $580,000 was stolen via this scheme. Sherman collected $82,500 in kickbacks from his friends.

(Continued)

Fraud Part 2. Sherman submitted a bogus invoice for $200,000 from a legitimate travel agent. He authorized payment of the invoice, which was to be paid via check to an address, which was not that of the travel agent, but belonged to one of Sherman's friends. The friend attempted to deposit the check in an account he fraudulently established in the name of the travel agent. The bank rejected the deposit, prompting Sherman to deceive the travel agent by claiming that he had in fact authorized his company to pay $200,000 to replenish his travel account in anticipation of "costly upcoming travel plans," but that the check mistakenly got attached to some paperwork that was sent to Texas. To cover his tracks, Sherman asked the agent to issue an invoice of $200,000, supposedly to "correct" the error.

Result. Sherman's company ended up making *two* $200,000 payments on two bogus invoices. When the travel agent informed Sherman that his employer had made two payments of $200,000, Sherman instructed them to deposit all $400,000 in an account he controlled. Fortunately, the company discovered the fraud before Sherman could steal the funds.

How could this fraud have been prevented? List as many controls as you can. Compare yours with those listed in Appendix B.

1. _____

2. _____

3. _____

▶ Review Points

- Prevention is always more effective and less costly than fraud *detection*. However prevention is not always possible. As a result, *detection* is essential.

- Basic detection techniques and procedures typically involve screening for operational fraud and involve manual, nonauditing measures. Detailed detection is designed for catching financial frauds such as those whose red flags are found in the organization's financial records and statements.

- Research has proven that employees who have a confidential hotline at their disposal and who are trained in the red flags of fraud are very likely to report such red flags when they identify them.

- Internal auditors should practice professional skepticism in determining the existence and seriousness of fraud risks in their regular internal audits.

- In ratio analysis of the organization's financial records, anomalies that are found from one accounting period to the next in key financial ratios provide reason to dig deeper for hard evidence of fraud.

- One of the most important basic fraud detection techniques that all divisions of your organization should implement is regular physical inventory checks—together with complete record keeping.
- Vendor fraud comes in so many varieties that they are often very difficult to detect. However, there *are* effective basic detection methods that should be followed at all times.

▶ Chapter Quiz

True or False:

1. Internal auditors are increasingly expected by management to detect fraud at both the basic *and* detailed level.
   - ❏ True   ❏ False

2. The most effective anonymous hotlines are ones operated by third-party vendors.
   - ❏ True   ❏ False

3. Surprise audits are effective in catching fraud, but not deterring it.
   - ❏ True   ❏ False

Circle the correct answer to the following questions:

4. An effective and efficient way to detect payroll fraud is:
   - a. Manually review all canceled paychecks
   - b. Do a periodic, unannounced manual distribution of paychecks
   - c. Look for paychecks of employees with similar surnames

5. To effectively detect vendor/billing fraud:
   - a. Periodically examine the details and billing/payment patterns of your largest vendor accounts
   - b. Investigate all vendor checks that are returned due to a wrong address
   - c. Manually review all vendor invoices to screen for signs of falsification

Fill in the blank:

6. Fraud prevention is always the most cost-effective way to reduce fraud losses. But because prevention is not always possible, _____ is essential.
7. Internal auditors should adopt a mindset of _____ in determining the existence or seriousness of fraud during their regular audits.

8. Surveillance using closed circuit cameras can be effective in detecting "_____ fraud."

9. Among the most important tools for enabling employees to report signs of fraud or suspicious activity is a _____.

For the answers, please turn to Appendix A.

CHAPTER EIGHT

Advanced Fraud Detection Tools and Techniques

The fraud risk assessment (FRA) described in Chapter 6 is not the *only* option available to you for identifying fraud risks in your organization. There are in fact many varieties of FRAs that organizations of all kinds use. Some are more effective than others. The one described in this workbook, however, has been used by large numbers of organizations with considerable documented success.

Key lesson. Regardless of the type of FRA you use, if properly executed, it will provide you with a list of fraud schemes and scenarios that are likeliest to occur in different operational sectors of your organization. The important thing to remember is this: If you determine through your FRA that there are specific areas where fraud *could* occur, you must adjust your audit procedures to dig deeper.

Important. These procedures go *beyond* the basic fraud detection methods described Chapter 7. In essence, they *augment* those procedures.

Critical FRA perspective. At this juncture it is also important to recall that it is impossible to *prevent* all fraud, which, as discussed earlier, is why we must devote substantial resources to *detection*. This provides an important additional perspective to the FRA. Not only is the FRA conducted for the purpose of identifying the specific risks of fraud so management can formulate and implement better *preventive* controls, it also serves the critical function of guiding auditors to *detecting* the detailed signs of fraud so that investigative or other action can be taken at management's discretion.

This chapter describes the key *advanced* audit methods for digging out these detailed indicators of fraud. They also allow you to make the critical distinction between evidence of honest human error and potential or actual fraud.

► Internal Audit and the Audit Plan

According to ACFE-IIA-AICPA's *The Business Risk of Fraud,*

> Internal auditors should consider the organization's assessment of fraud risk when developing their annual audit plan and periodically assess management's

fraud-detection capabilities. They should also interview and regularly communicate with those conducting the assessments, as well as others in key positions throughout the organization, to help them assess whether all fraud risks have been considered. When performing engagements, internal auditors should devote sufficient time and attention to evaluating the design and operation of internal controls related to preventing and detecting significant fraud risks. They should exercise professional skepticism when reviewing activities to be on guard for the signs of potential fraud. Potential frauds uncovered during an engagement should be treated in accordance with a well-defined response plan consistent with professional and legal standards.[1]

Important. This is a useful broad framework for your internal auditors and financial managers for applying the findings of their FRA to the adjustment of their audit procedures to detect specific red flags of fraud. However, to truly screen for fraud hidden in the organization's books and records, you must adopt rigorous *detailed* fraud auditing practices and techniques.

Among the most helpful guides for planning a detailed audit to detect fraud is *SAS 99*. As discussed in Chapter 7, basic fraud detection techniques include performing certain analyses of financial ratios. For perspective on why doing these analyses is important but insufficient for getting the full picture of fraud risks, *SAS 99* tells us:

> Analytical procedures performed during planning may be helpful in identifying the risks of material misstatement due to fraud. However, because such analytical procedures generally use data aggregated at a high level, the results of those analytical procedures provide only a broad initial indication about whether a material misstatement of the financial statements may exist. Accordingly, the results of analytical procedures performed during planning should be considered *along with other information gathered by the auditor in identifying the risks of material misstatement due to fraud* (emphasis added).[2]

Note. As indicated in this citation, *SAS 99* was formulated with the aim of detecting fraud that has a direct impact on "material misstatement." Essentially this means that anything in the organization's financial activities that could result in fraud-related misstatements in its financial records should be audited for by using *SAS 99* as a guide.

Critical. The fraud-auditing procedures of *SAS 99*—or of any other reputable guidance—will assist the auditor's efforts to distinguish between actual fraud and error. The two can often have similar characteristics, with the key difference being that of the existence or absence of *intent.*

Toward this end, *SAS 99* and other key fraud-auditing guidelines, provide detailed procedures for gathering evidence of potential fraud based on the lists of fraud risks resulting from your FRA:

> *SAS 99* was designed as a fraud-auditing tool for *external* auditors. However, since its inception in 2002, internal auditors in many organizations have been adopting several key fraud-auditing measures outlined in the document. In addition, *SAS 99* does strongly recommend direct involvement by internal auditors in the organization's fraud-auditing efforts: "Internal auditors may conduct proactive auditing to

search for corruption, misappropriation of assets, and financial statement fraud. This may include the use of computer-assisted audit techniques to detect particular types of fraud. Internal auditors also can employ analytical and other procedures to isolate anomalies and perform detailed reviews of high-risk accounts and transactions to identify potential financial statement fraud. The internal auditors should have an independent reporting line directly to the audit committee, enabling them to express any concerns about management's commitment to appropriate internal controls or to report suspicions or allegations of fraud involving senior management.[3]

Specifically, *SAS 99* provides a set of "audit responses" that are designed to gather hard evidence of potential fraud that could exist based what you learned from your FRA. Accordingly:

- The *nature* of auditing procedures performed may need to be changed to obtain evidence that is more reliable or to obtain additional corroborative information.

- The *timing* of substantive tests may need to be modified. The auditor might conclude that substantive testing should be performed at or near the end of the reporting period to best address an identified risk of material misstatement due to fraud.

- The *extent* of the procedures applied should reflect the assessment of the risks of material misstatement due to fraud. For example, increasing sample sizes or performing analytical procedures at a more detailed level may be appropriate.[4]

▶ Essentials of Fraud Auditing

SAS 99 provides some useful examples of how a detailed fraud-related response to specific risks determined by your FRA should be handled. In the case of fraudulent revenue recognition, for example, *SAS 99* recommends the following detailed audit steps:

> Because revenue recognition is dependent on the particular facts and circumstances, as well as accounting principles and practices that can vary by industry, the auditor ordinarily will develop auditing procedures based on [his or her] understanding of the entity and its environment, including the composition of revenues, specific attributes of the revenue transactions, and unique industry considerations. If [your FRA has identified a risk] of material misstatement due to fraud that involves improper revenue recognition, the auditor also may want to consider:
>
> - Performing substantive analytical procedures relating to revenue using disaggregated data, for example, comparing revenue reported by month and by product line or business segment during the current reporting period with comparable prior periods.
>
> - [Using computer-assisted audit techniques] in identifying unusual or unexpected revenue relationships or transactions (see the section below, "Essentials of Automated Auditing").
>
> - Confirming with customers . . . relevant contract terms and the absence of side agreements, because the appropriate accounting often is influenced by such terms or agreements. For example, acceptance criteria, delivery and payment terms, the absence of future or continuing vendor obligations, the right to return the product,

guaranteed resale amounts, and cancellation or refund provisions often are relevant in such circumstances.

- Inquiring of the entity's sales and marketing personnel or in-house legal counsel regarding sales or shipments near the end of the period and their knowledge of any unusual terms or conditions associated with these transactions.

- Being physically present at one or more locations at period-end to observe goods being shipped or being readied for shipment (or returns awaiting processing) and performing other appropriate sales and inventory cutoff procedures.

- For those situations for which revenue transactions are electronically initiated, processed, and recorded, testing controls to determine whether they provide assurance that recorded revenue transactions occurred and are properly recorded.[5]

Other useful fraud-auditing guidelines based on the results of an organization's FRA are provided by several resources, including CCH, a leading publisher of tax and business law information and software solutions, the American Institute of Certified Public Accountants (AICPA), the Association of Certified Fraud Examiners (ACFE), the Institute of Internal Auditors (IIA), and others. Here are some of the key widely accepted fraud-auditing techniques to use in following up on the findings of your FRA.

■ Auditing for Fraud in Accounts Payable

If your FRA reveals that there is a significant risk of fraud in the accounts payable (AP) function, auditors must adjust their audit plan and apply professional skepticism to audit for red flags of the specific AP-related frauds that could occur. *Such frauds often include:*

- Unauthorized purchases are made by employees.

- Purchases are recorded but goods or services are not received.

- Phony invoices are submitted.

- Purchase amounts are recorded falsely or incorrectly.

- Purchases are charged to the wrong account or recorded in the wrong period.

- Purchases are made on unfavorable terms such as inflated prices.

- Purchases are misclassified to conceal lack of authorization.

- Purchase discounts are taken but not recorded, and amounts of discounts are stolen.

- Improper deferrals of revenue are recorded in order to record income to future periods.

- Sales are fabricated or recorded before actually being concluded.

- Contingent liability is understated or not reflected in financial reports.

Use these fraud-related audit procedures to detect signs of AP fraud (or error):

- Send blank confirmations to vendors requesting them to furnish information about all outstanding invoices and other pertinent items such as payment terms, payment histories, and so forth. Include new vendors and accounts with small or zero balances.

- Confirm collectability of debit memos with vendors by calling the vendor.
- Match vendor names and addresses from invoices with Master Vendor List.
- Conduct Internet searches for vendor names and addresses to ensure the vendor and/or the address is valid.
- Look for paid invoices with no folds (most legitimate vendors send their invoices in a standard #10 envelope).
- Match approved vendor names and addresses with names and addresses of employees.
- Search for unusual or large year-end transactions and adjustments, such as transactions not containing normal processing initials, not going through normal processes, or not having normal supporting documentation.
- Review vendor files for unusual items, such as manually created and non-customized invoices, different delivery addresses, and vendors with multiple addresses.
- Examine disbursements made for services or other items that do not require delivery of goods.
- Examine voided checks for signs of fabrication or alteration.
- Examine supporting documents for payments of amounts just under the threshold required for approval or for dual signatures.
- Examine original canceled checks and scrutinize for items such as the following:
  - Discrepancies between canceled checks, invoices and the disbursements journal.
  - Multiple endorsements or forged endorsements.
  - The identity of the endorsees.
- Expand testing of receiving cutoff.
- Perform analytical procedures and predictive tests of key ratios (see Chapter 7).
- Search public records.
- Perform tests of controls over accounts payable and purchases.[6]

Auditing for Payroll Fraud

If your fraud risk assessment (FRA) reveals that there is a significant risk of payroll fraud, auditors must adjust their audit plan and apply professional skepticism to audit for red flags of these frauds.

Payroll fraud schemes are often in play when:

- Work is unauthorized or work that is not performed is accrued.
- Accrual of employee benefits—such as vacation pay, sick leave—is recorded but not earned, or is earned but not recorded.
- Terminated employees remain on the payroll.
- Fictitious employees (ghost employees) are on the payroll.

- Employees' earnings are overaccrued or underaccrued due to improper rates or computation errors.
- Employees receive unusually generous or unscheduled raises.
- Payroll expenses are recorded in the period paid rather than in the period earned.
- Time cards or hours-worked reports are fraudulently padded.

Use these fraud-related audit procedures to detect signs of payroll fraud (or error):

- Analyze payroll distributions over several pay periods.
- Follow up on payroll checks that have not been cashed.
- Conduct an unannounced distribution of paychecks, and require employees to present identification to obtain their paychecks.
- Analyze payroll records for employees with minimal or no deductions.
- Analyze commission payment records for unusual amounts or recipients.
- Review personnel files for anomalies in compensation rates.
- Consider implementing continuous auditing to screen for potential payroll schemes.
- Apply Benford's Law to analyze payroll accounts.*
- Test sample payroll calculations and deductions.
- Confirm amounts paid to employees working at home or at remote locations without direct supervision.
- Examine payroll disbursements subsequent to year-end and compare with accrued payroll at the balance-sheet date.
- Analyze payroll registers and the payroll check registers for unusual items such as names of former employees, duplicate employee names, duplicate employee addresses, unusual pay rates, unusual number of hours worked, and matching Social Security numbers for two different employees.
- Compare your list of current employees in the personnel department to the payroll journal.
- Analyze payroll data for unusual pay rates or number of hours worked.
- Examine canceled payroll checks for suspected fictitious employees.
- Perform tests of existing controls over payroll transactions.[7]

The bottom line. Once your auditors (external, internal, or a team comprising members of both) have completed these and other detailed tests to screen for fraud, you will end up with a clear body of red flags and hard evidence of potential frauds that management can then use to decide whether to launch a full-scale fraud investigation.

---

*Benford's Law analysis is a process of comparing actual results vs. expected results by looking for unusual transactions that do not fit an expected pattern.

While many auditors feel most comfortable conducting these transaction analyses manually or with Excel spreadsheets, the good news is that there are highly effective and affordable audit software programs available that enable you to perform most of these key fraud analyses much more efficiently. These programs perform what is called *audit analytics*, which refers to data analysis designed for audit and fraud detection.

Key. A major reason that many organizations use audit analytics today is that no system of internal anti-fraud controls is perfect and that means fraudsters will find the loopholes to enable them to commit crimes. Audit analytics software monitors internal controls to pinpoint deviations from normal financial operations that can be evidence of fraud.

Bottom line. Using such popular audit analytics software tools as ACL and IDEA, you can convert data from your organization's databases to information that is useful in gathering evidence of fraud.

Example. Let's say your FRA indicated a risk of, among other things, procurement fraud. As discussed in Chapter 6, one of the brightest red flags of this crime is setting up sham corporations. Using ACL or IDEA, you can specifically search for red flags of these such as:

- Two contractors have common names, with the first two letters of the names always the same, pointing to the possible existence of sham corporations, such as:

  - Two or more suppliers have the same telephone number or address.

  - Matching of vendors paid with the Vendor Master File reveals vendors that do not exist.

  - An employee and a "vendor" have the same demographics (address or phone number).

  - Checks paid to the "vendor" are always for even amounts, such as $2,000, $3,000, $8,000.

  - Employees in the payroll master file with no Social Security number, the same social security numbers, or the same demographics (address or phone number).

Even better. Custom-built programming scripts that run on your organization's servers. They usually cost more than off-the-shelf products like ACL and IDEA. However, they usually are much more effective in identifying accounting anomalies and patterns that support your suspicions of fraud based on the red flags that your FRA directed your attention to.[8]

Important. It is *not* the auditors' or fraud examiner's decision to launch a full-scale fraud investigation. Though the fraud-audit procedures described above may provide management with an abundant supply of evidence to go after suspected fraudsters, the decision to do so depends on more than just the results of the fraud audit. It often involves judgments about the cost, repercussions from publicity regarding the investigation and prospective prosecution of suspect(s) and the availability of experienced and qualified investigators to conduct such a probe.

Many anti-fraud experts argue that management should never let a suspected fraud go unaddressed. They suggest that not only does this send a message to other employees that management does not take fraud seriously enough to investigate and prosecute, it also perpetuates the widely held misconception that fraud is a victimless crime. Though the theft of a few thousand dollars by an employee with serious personal financial problems may not make a significant difference in the organization's financial performance, letting the perpetrator off the hook by simply terminating employment conveys the attitude that fraud is simply a cost of doing business or that it does not pay to prosecute.

Others would disagree, arguing that companies, law enforcement, and the judicial system have been comparatively lenient on white-collar criminals, and that this is a key reason we are seeing more and more fraud in our corporate, financial, governmental, and nonprofit institutions.

Hopefully, the information contained in this workbook has provided you with a foundation of knowledge from which to draw your own conclusions about the seriousness of the fraud problem in our economy and whether more should be done to detect and prevent it.

Remember

It is *management's* job to determine if a fraud investigation is required—not the auditor's, financial manager's, or controller's.

▶ Review Points

- At the detailed level of fraud detection, you must know what types of fraud to be on the lookout for before you can screen for evidence.

- The FRA assesses the *likelihood* that each of those frauds might occur and provides guidance on how to adjust audit procedures to screen for detailed indicators of fraud.

- Detailed fraud auditing techniques can be found in *SAS 99*, which is based on the concept of auditing for risks of fraud that result in material misstatements.

- Your FRA serves a *dual* purpose: (1) to identify the key fraud risks threatening your organization so that management can enhance the *preventive* controls necessary to reduce these risks and (2) to guide auditors in adjusting their audit plans so they can conduct detailed auditing techniques for *detecting* evidence of specific frauds.

- *SAS 99*, while initially designed for external auditors, also sets out a specific fraud-auditing role of internal auditors.

- The results of detailed fraud auditing should be immediately reported to management, whose job it is to determine whether a full-fledged fraud investigation is called for.

True or False:

1. Fraud risk assessments (FRAs) are typically conducted by an organization's external auditors—not its internal auditors.

❑ True   ❑ False

2. *SAS 99* was formulated with the main purpose of guiding auditors to detect accounts payable fraud.

❑ True   ❑ False

3. According to recent research, internal auditors should *not* get involved in the evaluation of the organization's internal controls.

❑ True   ❑ False

Circle the correct answer to the following questions:

4. Adjusting audit plans to the findings of an FRA requires:

    a. Implementing a continuous inventory monitoring program

    b. Conducting surprise audit procedures such as counting cash at specific organization locations

    c. Discussing with management the best audit procedures for finding evidence of frauds, which, according to the FRA, the organization is particularly vulnerable to

5. Which of the following is *not* one of the potential audit responses indicated by the results of your FRA?

    a. The nature of audit procedures

    b. The timing of a substantive test

    c. The frequency of audit procedures

    d. The extent of testing

6. The decision whether to conduct a full-scale fraud investigation rests with which of the following?

    a. External auditors

    b. Internal auditors

    c. Senior management

    d. Corporate counsel

Fill in the blank:

7. One of the key exercises in a FRA is determining the _____ of specific fraud schemes or scenarios occurring.

8. When auditing for fraud, it is important to make the distinction between fraud and _____.

9. One of the key objectives of auditing for fraud is to gather sufficient evidence to enable management to determine whether or not to initiate a _____.

10. A full-fledged fraud investigation should not be conducted by an auditor. It should be conducted by a specialist in this practice, such as a _____.

For the answers, please turn to Appendix A.

◀ **APPENDIX A** ▶

Answers to Chapter Quizzes

▶ **Chapter 1: Why No Organization Is Immune to Fraud**

1. T
2. T
3. F
4. c
5. c
6. b
7. d
8. tone at the top
9. report
10. code of conduct

▶ **Chapter 2: The Human Element of Fraud**

1. T
2. T
3. c
4. c
5. d
6. c
7. Report
8. supervisor
9. soft

▶ **Chapter 3: Employee-Level Fraud**

1. T, T, F, T
2. T, F, T, T

3. T, T, F, F

4. T, T, T, F

5. d

6. c

7. a

8. a

9. c

10. b

11. c

12. c

13. Yes, Yes, No, Yes

14. Yes, No, Yes, No

15. b

16. b

17. ghost

18. identity theft

19. altering sensitive documents

▶ Chapter 4: Management-Level Fraud

1. T

2. F

3. T

4. b

5. a

6. d

7. b

8. c

9. Cash

10. Personal use

11. Misuse of assets

12. a, b

13. b

14. b

▶ Chapter 5: External Fraud

1. T: Stealing is correct because the unknown vendor may be someone outside the company—probably a dishonest employee of the vendor—submitting phony

invoices to divert company checks to her own address. Conning is incorrect because no lies or false excuses are being offered to commit the fraud. Altering is incorrect because the invoice has been created from scratch, not altered. Misrepresenting is correct because the person who prepared the invoice is misrepresenting herself as a legitimate vendor.

2. F: Stealing is correct because the new employee is stealing money from the company by preparing inaccurate expense reports. Conning is correct because the employee is attempting to persuade his employer that his phony expenses are legitimate. Altering is incorrect because the employee is not altering expense reports—he is creating them himself. Misrepresenting is correct because the employee's impressive resume was probably embellished to conceal previous illegal activity.

3. T: Stealing is correct because if successful, the fraudster will end up having misappropriated your organization's funds. Conning is correct because the fraudster is attempting gain the target employee's confidence in order to carry out the scheme. Altering is incorrect because no documents or other files are being changed as part of the scheme. Misrepresenting is correct because the fraudster is lying to the employee about who he really is.

4. d

5. a, b, d

6. c

7. engineering

8. e-mail

9. misrepresentation

10. vendor

▶ Chapter 6: Conducting a Successful Fraud Risk Assessment

1. T

2. T

3. F

4. F

5. b

6. b

7. risk

8. internal controls

9. brainstorming

10. material

▶ Chapter 7: Basic Fraud Detection Tools and Techniques

1. T

2. T
3. F
4. b
5. a
6. detection
7. professional skepticism
8. physical
9. confidential hotline

▶ Chapter 8: Advanced Fraud Detection Tools and Techniques

1. T
2. F
3. F
4. c
5. c
6. c
7. risk
8. error
9. fraud investigation
10. certified fraud examiner

Answer Key for Case Studies

▶ Case Study #1: Pain, Pills, and Petty Cash

■ You've probably heard the term "segregation of duties." In this case, Deena's bookkeeping duties should have been separated—by having someone *other than Deena* approve Petty Cash outlays as well as reconciling bank statements.

■ Deena's boss should have seen the declining quality of her work as a red flag and questioned her about possible personal problems or other pressures.

■ The organization should not have allowed checks to be made out to cash, or if it did, it should have required all such checks to be signed by two authorized signatories.

▶ Case Study #2: The Trusted Thief

■ *Segregation of duties*: Scott should *not* have been allowed to process invoices, make checks, send them out, and make entries into the financial records.

■ Apparently no one at Harvest House or its Board reconciled the organization's bank statements for three years. This lack of financial control allowed Scott to get away with his fraud.

■ More frequent audits—at least once a year, with a focus on detecting signs of fraud.

■ Surprise audits.

■ A surprise manual distribution of payroll checks by an auditor to see if any checks were not legitimate.

▶ Case Study #3: Demise by Personal Debt

■ Tighter scrutiny by the organization's board.

■ Implementation of a board policy on use of business credit cards—including spending limits.

- Training of employees to detect and report signs of fraud.
- Regular audits of the organization's financial records—including, especially, the executives' credit card statements.

▶ Case Study #4: Shell Game in the Big Apple

- Have the Board of Directors assess internal controls over financial reporting and investigate suspicious financial numbers.
- Require management to implement and monitor the effectiveness of new internal controls over financial reporting.
- Have internal audit investigate any transactions that appear unusual or suspicious.
- Implement a whistle-blower hotline, and encourage employees to use it to report suspicious financial activity.
- Ensure that internal and external auditors examine unusual or suspicious transactions recorded at the end of a reporting period.
- Tighten controls over the Vendor Master File—to verify that all approved vendors are real—rather than shell companies.

▶ Case Study #5: Health Care Fraud

- Implement and monitor the effectiveness of accounts payable scrutiny of all purchase orders to screen for anomalies or other signs of potential falsification.
- Match all deliveries with applicable purchase orders—without exception.
- Tighten controls over the Vendor Master File—to verify that all approved vendors are real—rather than shell companies.
- Implement a whistle-blower hotline, and encourage employees to use it to report suspicious financial activity.
- Enforce limitations on employee access to the organization's secure computer systems. Regularly assess the effectiveness of these controls.

▶ Case Study #6: Robbing Peter to Pay Paul

- Have a second employee involved in counting and verifying incoming receipts.
- Monitor receivables closely.
- Check to be sure cash deposits are equal to cash receipts.
- Investigate if you have complaints from vendors who say they have not received credit for their payments.
- Make photocopies of the front and back of all incoming checks, and be sure they are deposited into the proper bank account.

► Case Study #7: Kickbacks Fly When Controls Are Weak

- Assign a procurement or accounts payable (AP) staff member who is independent of specific vendor relationships or transactions to approve large-dollar purchases.
- Require AP to investigate any sudden price increases in items ordered.
- Enforce requirements for disclosure of managers' financial interests as control against conflict of interest.
- Implement and monitor the effectiveness of AP scrutiny of all purchase orders to screen for anomalies or other signs of potential falsification.
- Separate duties of purchasing and invoice approval.
- Review and, if necessary, improve controls over competitive bidding procedures.

► Case Study #8: Wining and Dining on Customer Dollars

- Require expense reports to include full descriptions of the business purpose of each expense, the original receipt or other support documentation, time and date, location, and exact amount.
- Be suspicious of rounded dollar numbers without supporting documentation or potentially counterfeit documentation, as well as a series of expenses for the same amount.
- Have receipts cross-referenced to the expense report and sent directly to the processing group.
- Monitor and *enforce* per diem expense policies. This will result in flagging excessive expenses when reimbursement claims are reviewed for approval.

► Case Study #9: The New Employee

- *Segregation of duties*: Suzanne should not be both the bookkeeper and the payroll administrator. Also—the payroll administrator should *not* be the person doing payroll bank reconciliations.
- Internal audit should regularly review payroll records for more than one employee with the same address, more than one employee with the same identification information and, employees with *suspicious* addresses.
- Allow addition of new employees to the payroll *only* if an authorized manager gives written approval.
- Allow addition of new employees only if *two* authorized managers provide written approval.
- Do background checks on all new hires.

► Case Study #10: Information Is as Good as Gold

- Tighten controls—over who gets access to secure data. Require "special" access to be approved by more than one authorized IT manager.
- Closely monitor compliance with these controls.
- Implement clear controls over the types of projects and purposes for which confidential information can be used.
- Implement specific classification of what *types* of information are considered sensitive and which are less sensitive.
- Implement and enforce information security policies, including listings of prohibited information-related activities.

► Case Study #11: But She Was Such a Nice Lady!

- Tighten control over access to highly sensitive computer systems and databases, especially those storing financial files.
- Conduct thorough background checks prior to offering a finance-related job. Look for prior criminal activity or irresponsible personal financial conduct.
- Implement the same controls and reviews as discussed in earlier sections on embezzlement and check fraud.

► Case Study #12: Brenda Belton's Conflict of Interest Scheme

- Verify check payees against Vendor Master File.
- *Segregation of duties*: The bank statements should be reviewed and reconciled by an independent AP staffer.
- Implement detailed review of invoices by purchasing/procurement staff. This would have revealed that "vendor" addresses were suspicious.
- Implement stringent controls over contract awarding to prevent nonbidding.
- Enforcement policies requiring financial disclosure by executives to screen for potentially problematic financial interests on the part of managers or executives.

► Case Study #13: The Great Buca Restaurant Fraud

- Require active audit committee oversight of internal controls over financial reporting, including, if appropriate, conducting independent reviews of compliance with rules governing internal controls over financial reporting. Require audit committee review and reporting on tone at the top.
- Train internal auditors to detect red flags of fraudulent financial reporting.

- Implement a whistle-blower hotline and train all employees and managers in how to use it and inform them of the legal protections for whistle-blowers against retaliation or retribution.

▶ Case Study #14: The Phoner Toner Scam

- Require only designated employees to approve orders from outside vendors.
- Compare the caller's company name against your organization's approved vendor list.
- Train employees to be aware of this scheme, and ask them to tell callers they will call back after checking with their supervisor.

▶ Case Study #15: The Frito Fraud

- Never—ever—execute a disbursement on the strength of an e-mail alone. Full and detailed person-to-person and properly authorized changes to any payment arrangement must be required and monitored.
- Immediately notify the proper authorizing manager of receipt of any communication from a vendor or other payee. The manager in turn should approve transactions *only* if all required documentation is supplied.
- Approve disbursements to a vendor's "new" bank account only following authentication of the new account's owner.
- Make disbursements to new accounts only after official, written, and signed requests from the vendor are received and verbal (telephone or in-person) verification of the change has been made.

▶ Case Study #16: I'm the Boss, and I Can Use Any Vendors I Want

- Segregate Sherman's duties by prohibiting him from approving invoices and having them processed by the AP department.
- Examine the legitimacy of all new vendors by verifying their addresses and licenses and checking them against the Vendor Master File.
- Have at least two managers approve all travel-related disbursements.
- Require dual approval of all disbursements over a specified amount.

An Introduction to Cyber Fraud

▶ Introduction

This Workbook has, it is hoped, provided you with a solid foundation of knowledge about the main types of internal and external fraud threatening most organizations today.

Throughout the book, you saw brief references to the issue of electronic data security—as it relates to use in such frauds as extortion, identity fraud, and manipulation of the organization's electronic data and records.

An important closing message. Due to the incredibly rapid advances in technology and electronic communications, a steadily increasing proportion of total fraud is being perpetrated with the use of computers, the Internet, and sophisticated software and programming techniques.

This will require all of us to enhance our familiarity with the high-tech methods being used more and more by both internal and external fraudsters.

While some of the detection and prevention methods for managing these cyber risks will be technological, a human element in the fight against cyber fraud will always be central to the war on such crimes.

The following pages contain a series of discussions on current issues in cyber fraud. Together they offer a useful overview of the problem and practical methods for detecting and preventing these crimes.

▶ Major Cyber-Fraud Threats

■ Cyber Criminals Becoming More Aggressive

Cyber criminals are reducing the time it takes to launch computer attacks that take advantage of publicly disclosed security holes. According to IBM's latest Internet Security Systems XForce report, there are two growing trends in Internet threats:

1. Online criminals' use of programs that help them automatically generate attacks based on publicly available information about vulnerabilities. In the past they spent more time finding those security holes themselves. Now finding them is no longer required; it occurs automatically.

2. Quicker and increasingly detailed release by security researchers of information relating to newly discovered software flaws.

Details. Though researchers have typically waited until the affected company has released a software patch before revealing details, increasingly they are releasing not only details of the vulnerability but also proof-of-concept exploit code to show that the flaw is legitimate.

Problem. This gives criminals a framework for creating new cyber attacks.

Example. In Web browsers, hacking exploits are now available within one day after flaws are discovered 94 percent of the time—up from 79 percent in 2007.

White-Collar Crime Fighter **source.** IBM Internet Security Systems Xforce report, cited in the *Cyber Crime Newsletter*, a bimonthly publication developed under the Cyber Crime Training Partnership between the National Association of Attorneys General (NAAG) and the National Center for Justice and the Rule of Law (NCJRL) at the University of Mississippi School of Law. The newsletter is written and edited by Hedda Litwin, Cyber Crime Counsel.

■ Computer Fraud: Understanding the True Nature of the Insider Threat

For decades, computer security specialists have spent the lion's share of their budgets hardening their organizations' defenses against external fraud and cyber-crime threats.

Most common. Viruses, worms, Trojan horses, keyloggers, and other common forms of malicious attack that resulted in either system sabotage, theft of confidential information, or diversion of the organization's financial assets or those of its customers. Only in the past few years has it become abundantly clear that insiders are equally if not more serious fraud threats to their employers than outsiders.

Result. Today, any organization lacking a stringent set of internal computer security policies, processes, and procedures to counter the numerous threats of insider fraud puts itself at serious risk of financial and reputational damage, as well as legal and/or regulatory repercussions in the event of a successful insider attack.

The good news. While monitoring and assessing insider computer fraud risks is potentially complex and costly—as are the identification and implementation of optimal antifraud technology, policies, and procedures—understanding the actual nature of the insider computer fraud threat is surprisingly simple. *Key concepts.*

- The term *trusted insider* includes employees, former employees, contractors, consultants, service providers, software vendors, and so on. Any of these parties can be potential abusers of your computer system to perpetrate diversion of funds in a host of ways.

- Key elements of computer fraud include:
  - Accessing or using a computer without authorization, or by exceeding authorization.

- Accessing or using a computer with the intent to commit a fraudulent or other criminal act. "Other criminal act" can refer to illegally obtaining restricted data or confidential financial information, or damaging or destroying information contained in a computer.

Common Forms of Computer Fraud

According to key research, the varieties of computer fraud are equally straightforward. They fall into three main categories:

1. **Input transaction manipulation schemes.** *These include:*

   - *Extraneous transactions.* These are illegal transactions initiated by a trusted insider, such as unauthorized billing transactions that result in disbursement of company funds to the perpetrator or a shell company he or she controls. These frauds can also involve manipulating the organization's computer data pertaining to one or more customers, vendors, products, accounting entries, salespeople, and so on that the perpetrator exploits at a later time.

   - *Failure to enter transactions.* This is a common technique in many billing schemes.

     Examples: A purchasing associate who is perpetrating a billing scheme can intentionally prevent a bogus invoice from being entered into the payments system. Or a staffer responsible for accounts receivable can neglect to credit an account when payment is received (see also following discussion).

   - *Transaction modification.* Also common in billing schemes or collusion, these involve fraudulently increasing or reducing amounts charged to a particular account.

   - *Misuse of adjustment transactions.* Computer systems for legitimately correcting accounting errors or to record adjustments to inventory loss or spoilage can be abused by employees with access to such systems by falsifying entries to cover up outright theft or more elaborate billing schemes. *Related schemes:* Entering fraudulent error corrections or intentionally omitting such corrections to conceal fraud.

2. **Unauthorized program modification schemes.** This category of computer-generated insider schemes typically involves making unauthorized changes to automated payment or accounting software programs. A common form of this crime involves programming the system to execute high numbers of mini frauds such as rounding of numbers, fraudulently adding service charges, or diverting amounts of money so small as to fall below the radar of internal controls on accounts owned by the fraudster. *Additional varieties:*

   - *Processing undocumented transaction codes.* By manipulating the payments system to accept undocumented, false transaction codes for small transactions in situations where controls are absent, the fraudster can program the system to process fraudulent transactions that are entered directly by the perpetrator or by the computer via unauthorized programming changes.

- *Balance manipulation.* Here a dishonest internal computer programmer alters specific programs in a way that fraudulently forces account balances, in order to conceal embezzlement or other types of fraud that would otherwise be detectable by auditors.

- *Lapping schemes.* An insider with authorization to utilize the organization's automated accounting system can steal incoming payments and credit them to his or her own account and then manipulate the system to fraudulently credit the intended payee's account with a payment subsequently received from another account. The process is repeated until, due to slipup in timing or sharp auditing, the scheme is detected.

- *Fraudulent file modifications.* These crimes involve secretly changing account status through basic computer programming.

  Examples: Opening a fraudulent new account to receive automatic payments from payroll, retirement, unemployment, or welfare systems, destroying records of a fraudulent account, or fraudulently increasing a credit limit on a revolving credit line.

3. **File alteration and substitution schemes.** *Common examples:*

   - *Accessing a live master file.* The internal fraudster accesses the file and, using a specially written program or a general retrieval program, makes fraudulent adjustments to the file, such as a Vendor Master File, by modifying account balances, altering a payee, changing supplier addresses, adding bogus vendors, and so on.

   - *Substitution of a dummy version of a real file.* The fraudster initiates the scheme by obtaining access to the master file and then uses a special computer program to run the legitimate master file in order to create a duplicate. However, the duplicate has a few modifications when it is substituted for the legitimate file, thereby enabling the fraudster to hide fraudulent transactions that would otherwise be detected.

White-Collar Crime Fighter source. *Inside Computer Fraud: An In-Depth Framework for Detecting and Defending Against Insider IT Attacks,* by Kenneth C. Brancik, PhD, CISA, CISSP, ITIL, a former regulator at the Federal Reserve Bank of New York. Dr. Brancik currently works for a large U.S. defense contractor. He can be reached via the book's publisher, Auerbach Publications (www.auerbach-publications.com). Used by permission.

■ Disturbing News from the Underground Cyber-Crime Economy

According to the latest research from Symantec, the so-called underground cyber-crime economy is alive and flourishing, with organizations of various levels of sophistication and geographical reach aggressively advertising their fraudulent wares.

Of special concern to credit card issuers and merchants. Of all items for illegal sale and purchase on the Internet, stolen credit card information ranks at the top, representing 31 percent of all items sold and 24 percent of the total requested by prospective purchasers.

However, illegally obtained credit card information represents 59 percent of the total value of goods sold in the underground cyber economy.

Important. That total—$276 million—does not account for the amount of losses attributable to fraudulent use of the cyber contraband, such as maxing out of card accounts by end users of illegally obtained credit card information.

Following credit card information on the list are, respectively, financial account information (20 percent and 18 percent) and spam/phishing information (19 percent and 21 percent). Financial account information, according to Symantec, includes bank account credentials, magnetic stripe skimming devices, online payment services, online currency accounts, and online stock trading accounts.

White-Collar Crime Fighter source. *Symantec Report on the Underground Economy July 07–June 08*, published by Symantec.

▶ Cyber-Fraud Detection

■ Five Cyber Gold Mines for Finding Evidence of Fraud

Though e-mail evidence continues to play a powerful role in fraud investigations and litigation, technology is evolving in such a way that tech-savvy fraudsters are creating digital evidence in a variety of new formats. For attorneys and fraud investigators, this means searching for digital leads in the form of instant messages, Web content, metadata, and an expanding list of other sophisticated data formats. *When searching for cyber clues, fraud investigators and counsel should consider the following electronic gold mines:*

- **E-mails and attachments.** E-mails and attachments can be created and stored on operating systems, USB drives, PDAs, digital cameras, music players, and more. When seeking e-mail evidence, be sure to request attachments associated with an e-mail. In addition, inquire about e-mail storage conventions, such as limitations on mailbox sizes/storage locations, schedule and logs for storage, and so on. Also ask for any information relating to corporate e-mail retention, preservation, and destruction policies.

  E-mail evidence was instrumental in such high-profile fraud cases as those involving Bear Stearns in 2008, Citigroup analyst Jack Grubman in 2001, and Martha Stewart in 2002.

- **Web content.** From public Websites to intranets, portals, and extranets, potentially relevant data can exist all across the Web. The growing popularity of blogs and vlogs (blogs that use video as the primary medium for distributing content) also makes the Web a priceless data mine.

  Caution. When examining Web content, keep in mind that it may have dynamic features such as moving graphics and animations, sometimes rendering an automated capture that merely records screen shots insufficient for the investigation.

■ **Embedded data and metadata.** Embedded data, hidden and unavailable to computer users who are not technically adept, can be a significant form of evidence in a fraud case. Likewise, metadata—the data about the data—includes information about who created a file, the date it was created, and when it was last modified.

Example. In an e-mail message, metadata header information would likely include the e-mail's author, the list of addressees, and the date it was sent. Embedded data and metadata can reveal a computer user's conduct by leaving behind information about the history, tracking, or management of an electronic document.

■ **Instant messages.** Communicating via instant messaging (IM) has become the modern equivalent of watercooler conversations in the workplace. Unfortunately for some individuals who type and send messages they may have intended for off-the-record consumption by a co-worker, these conversations have the potential to be permanently preserved on a computer hard drive or IM archive. Depending on the instant messaging software used, these conversations may be recoverable. The growing number of companies logging and monitoring IM chat sessions makes the chances of obtaining evidence of fraudulent activity better than ever before.

■ **Emerging formats.** Animations, digital audio, video and audiovisual recordings, and digital voice e-mails are parts of a growing list of new formats that can store valuable electronic evidence. Electronic data created and stored in these unconventional formats is discoverable, and prosecutors and investigators should not hesitate to request such data if it is relevant to the case at hand.

White-Collar Crime Fighter **source.** Michele C.S. Lange, Esq., staff attorney, Kroll Ontrack, Inc., electronic discovery and computer forensics service providers.

■ Responding to Fraud: Teamwork Is Essential

When a fraud hits, the last thing you want to be doing is wasting precious time figuring out how to respond.

Reason. Frauds against corporations or other organizations are often complex, and it is usually impossible for one person to conduct an investigation single-handedly. Successful fraud investigations almost always require a team of qualified people who are prepared in advance to respond rapidly to allegations or indicators of fraud.

Key. To maximize the effectiveness of your fraud response team, start by identifying key team members and defining their specific responsibilities. Team members may be from both inside and outside of your organization, as some required skills might not be found among your existing staff.

Important. To avoid potential conflicts of interest in investigations, identify more than one qualified person to fill essential team positions.

Essential Fraud Response Team Members

Key members of an effective fraud response team should include the following:

- **Legal counsel.** Legal counsel is critical in any fraud response. It can be appropriate to use either internal or external counsel. However, for a greater degree of independence, consider retaining outside counsel to support investigation of particularly sensitive or significant frauds. *Reasons:*
    - Legal counsel should direct the investigation. This can be difficult for in-house counsel who are directly involved in many of the organization's policies and procedures.
    - Outside legal counsel can help address legal risks associated with fraud and its investigation.
    - Outside counsel can help keep sensitive information confidential by virtue of attorney-client privilege and attorney work product doctrine.

- **Management representative.** It is virtually impossible to conduct an effective fraud investigation without top management support. For this reason, a management representative—or, in significant cases, an audit committee or board member—should be part of your fraud response team. *Important:*
    - Ensure that the management representative is kept informed of all details of any investigation.
    - Require your management representative to provide all support and/or corporate resources necessary to complete an investigation.

- **Fraud investigator.** Fraud investigations typically require the input of an experienced financial professional with particular familiarity with the red flags of financial wrongdoing and how to detect them. Forensic accountants and auditors today have powerful software tools at their disposal when fraud investigations require their input. *Helpful:*

    A certified fraud examiner (CFE) can be ideal for this role. These professionals are trained to conduct complex fraud investigations from inception to resolution. If internal personnel can't fill the role of financial investigator, identify one or more outside fraud examiners or other financial crime investigation experts to support your company.

    Added advantage. Outside antifraud consultants may provide a greater degree of independence, objectivity, and experience in an investigation than a full-time employee. (For additional information, contact the Association of Certified Fraud Examiners at www.acfe.com.)

    Essential. Have legal counsel retain any outside investigator to maximize confidentiality protections under attorney-client privilege and attorney work product doctrine.

- **Computer forensic consultant.** Virtually every fraud investigation today depends—at least in part—on information and evidence collected from the victimized organization's computer systems.

Essential. To avoid inadvertently contaminating or altering key electronic evidence, it is critical that data collection and safeguarding be conducted by someone trained and experienced in computer forensics. *Also essential:*

- System and network administrators should not be used in this role. They are rarely well trained in computer forensic skills. For assistance in locating a qualified computer forensic expert, contact the International High Tech Crime Investigation Association (HTCIA) at www.htcia.org.

- As with a fraud investigator, have legal counsel retain any computer forensic consultant to maximize confidentiality protections.

- **Internal auditors.** Internal auditors are often valuable members of any fraud response team. *Reasons:*

  - Internal auditors may, during the course of their audits, be the first to uncover indicators of fraud and recommend a fraud investigation.

  - Internal auditors are familiar with controls and processes throughout the organization and can therefore lend critical insight into how a fraud occurred.

  - Internal auditors are often well qualified to perform fieldwork and detailed financial analysis for an investigation.

- **Information technology (IT) administrator.** IT administrators support fraud investigations by providing information on computer systems in use at the victimized organization: where information is stored and how data can be accessed. This information may be important to a computer forensic examination.

  Caution. IT administrators should generally *not* be directly involved in any fraud investigation since they usually lack investigative expertise.

- **Security representative.** Internal security personnel may have conventional investigative skills that prove valuable to a fraud investigation. They may, for example, be able to conduct interviews, obtain records, and perform other tasks in support of a fraud investigation.

  Caution. Security personnel usually lack the financial skills or experience to deal with complex frauds.

- **Human resources representative.** Consulting with an HR representative can help control some of the legal and regulatory risks associated with a fraud investigation. *Examples:*

  - An HR representative can help ensure that company policies and procedures are followed during any investigation.

  - The involvement of an HR representative at the appropriate time helps ensure that employee rights are not violated during the course of an investigation. He or she can also reduce the risk of wrongful-termination suits or other legal actions by employees.

  Caution. Due to their lack of investigative expertise, human resources personnel should not be directly involved in fraud investigations.

- **Public relations representative.** Given the risks associated with public disclosure of fraud, external communications about fraud impacting the company must be effectively planned and managed.

Effective. Experienced public relations professionals are invaluable in managing external communications and minimizing potential damage to your organization's reputation and brand.

White-Collar Crime Fighter **source.** Carl Lackstrom, CIA, CISSP, CFE, Associate Director, Protiviti, a leading business risk and internal audit firm, Boston, Massachusetts, www.protivit.com.

► Cyber-Fraud Prevention

■ Guarding against Newest Malware Threats

Malware is the term coined for malicious software designed by cyber criminals to damage a computer or network of computers. Malware comes in the form of viruses, worms, spyware, botnets, and other sinister-sounding cyber concoctions.

Important. Before use of the Internet became so widespread, most malware was created as pranks or vandalism. Now, however, malware makers are after big profits.

Example. Spyware is the term for malware programs that track the user's computing activities and secretly gather information for advertisers or other parties.

It is often installed without consent during another program download or when the user clicks on an untrustworthy pop-up window. Similarly, latest-generation Trojan horses are so sophisticated that the criminals who distribute them can use them to grab filled-out forms such as credit card applications, mortgage papers, and other documents containing confidential personal information—while the victim is completely oblivious to the theft.

Moreover, as companies store larger and larger amounts of customer information, those that are unprepared are at greater risk of a malware infection resulting in a data breach. Customer information in the hands of criminals results in costly identity fraud and equally burdensome damage control for targeted organizations. *Preventive basics:*

- Keep your operating system updated. With the millions of lines of code, it's foreseeable that a security vulnerability will exist that can be exploited by a malicious program writer.

- Install a firewall—it's a barrier that filters the information allowed into your system.

- Install the most up-to-date antivirus software available.

- Be prepared. No system is breach-proof. Recovery from such a disaster can be greatly facilitated if your organization regularly makes and maintains system backups.

White-Collar Crime Fighter **source.** Alan Brill, Senior Managing Director at Kroll Ontrack, computer security and forensics consultants in New York City.

■ Information Breach Solution: Incident Ownership

Common corporate mistake after an information breach is discovered: Failing to immediately make one competent manager fully accountable for remediation and provide him or her with the authority to execute all necessary actions.

Results. In a large organization, each business line will attempt to initiate its own remedial steps, and failure will result from lack of coordination.

Essential. The accountable manager must have the authority to force leaders from each business line to work under his or her lead to coordinate planning for a clear and efficient organization-wide response.

Important. Ensure that the manager in charge of response can require needed personnel such as IT security and other technology professionals to stick with the remediation program until it is complete. Often, companies ask these professionals for their help, but before the task is completed, they say their regular workload is piling up and they must excuse themselves.

Key. With a "throat to choke"—a person whom top management can put the screws to when a breach is discovered and urgent action is needed—the organization has the best chance of minimizing damage from a security incident.

White-Collar Crime Fighter **source.** Kevin Mandia of Mandiant Corporation, information security consultants, speaking at the Black Hat 2009 conference in Washington, D.C.

■ Secure Password Protection Essentials

The U.S. Cyber Consequences Unit (US-CCU), a nonprofit private research organization under contract to the Department of Homeland Security, recently completed a useful set of checklists for organizations to use in benchmarking or eliminating their vulnerabilities to cyber attacks.

Among the several especially useful checklists is the one pertaining to corporate management of passwords. The checklist uses a question format, indicating that any items to which the answer is "no" is in need of immediate attention. *Questions for minimizing password-related vulnerabilities to cyber attack:*

- Do corporate policies require secure procedures for issuing passwords?
- Do corporate policies define minimum password length requirements, taking into account the user's role as well as the password length that computer systems can support?
- Are applications that are developed within the organization protected by passwords with a minimum and maximum number of characters?
- Do policies set specific password complexity standards—such as requiring a mix of letters and numbers or characters chosen from large character sets?
- Are there policies and safeguards to prevent passwords from being transmitted in clear text via e-mail or instant messaging?
- Are employees required to change their passwords on a set schedule?
- Are employees prevented from using previously used passwords when a scheduled password change is required?
- Does the organization have technology in place to prevent passwords stored in encrypted or unencrypted files from being stolen?

- Are the organization's systems armed with alarm mechanisms that warn about the theft of a file containing a password?

- Is there a procedure for rapidly and securely changing passwords in the event that they are compromised?

- Does the company have—and enforce—a policy requiring immediate deactivation of passwords when an employee is terminated, leaves, or retires?

White-Collar Crime Fighter **source.** The US-CCU Cyber-Security Check List (2007), U.S. Cyber Consequences Unit.

■ Locking Down Laptops

With the multiple millions of dollars that organizations spend to blockade their networks against cyber thieves, it is strange that masses of confidential customer, employee, and intellectual information continue to be stolen by low-tech laptop thieves. *Here is one top security expert's formula for avoiding this costly crime:*

- Ensure that the laptop disk is encrypted.

- Enforce strong and complex password practices—to provide only authorized access to the system.

- Ensure single user login.

- Secure administrator access by using best practices standards.

- Lock down LAN settings on laptops.

- Maintain detailed records of your system information, such as MAC address, so that it is easy to trace a lost laptop on the Internet using available tools.

- Require employees to carry laptops in bags that aren't readily identifiable as laptop cases.

- Equip laptops with security tags embedded on the laptop body and that cannot be removed. This is useful in cases where the location of a stolen machine is known and where physical searches can identify the machine as belonging to your organization.

White-Collar Crime Fighter **source.** Krishnan Ramanathan, an experienced multinational corporate security professional. He currently is principal consultant at JP Adroit Consultants Private Limited, a firm in Bangalore, India, providing integrated risk management services, enterprise security solutions, financial due diligence, background verifications, investigations, and information and IT security solutions.

■ The Evolving IT Side of Fraud Prevention

The American Institute of Certified Public Accountants (AICPA), Institute of Internal Auditors (IIA), and Association of Certified Fraud Examiners (ACFE) released their *Managing the Business Risk of Fraud: A Practical Guide*, which provides a clear and succinct picture of the major policies, procedures, roles, and responsibilities of an organization to optimize its defenses against fraud.

Buried in the middle of the guide is a key section on the technological essentials of fraud prevention. The *Guide*'s uniquely nontechnical analysis of this issue may be of great value to management in all areas and at all levels. The following condensed excerpts of the IT component of fraud risk mitigation may be particularly useful to all. . . .

Today's global computer systems face an ongoing threat of cyber fraud that can result in significant financial and information losses.

Key. IT-related fraud risks include:

- Threats to data integrity.
- Threats from hackers to system security.
- Theft of financial and sensitive business information.

Important. These threats are not always restricted to abuse of information alone. Whether in the form of hacking, economic espionage, Web defacement, sabotage of data, viruses, or unauthorized access to data, IT can be used by people intent on committing fraud in any of the three key occupational fraud risk areas defined by the ACFE—fraudulent financial reporting, asset misappropriation, and corruption.[*] *Key risks in each category include:*

- **Fraudulent financial reporting:**
  - Unauthorized access to accounting applications—for example, personnel with inappropriate access to the general ledger, subsystems, or the financial reporting tool can post fraudulent entries.
  - Override of system controls. General computer controls include restricted system access, restricted application access, and program change controls. IT personnel may be able to access restricted data or fraudulently manipulate records.

- **Misappropriation of assets:**
  - *Theft of tangible assets.* Individuals who have access to tangible assets—cash, inventory, and fixed assets—and to the accounting systems that track and record activity related to those assets can use IT to conceal their thefts.
    Examples. A dishonest employee may establish a fictitious vendor in the Vendor Master File to facilitate the payment of phony invoices . . . or steal inventory and charge the cost of sales account for the stolen items, thus removing the asset from the balance sheet.
  - *Theft of intangible assets.* As Western economies are increasingly defined by their service sectors, more and more high-value assets of organizations are intangibles such as customer lists, proprietary business practices, copyrighted material, and other intellectual property. Examples of theft of intangible assets

---

*See the ACFE's 2008 *Report to the Nation on Occupational Fraud and Abuse*, www.acfe.com.

include hacking into large retail chains to steal customer credit card records and piracy of software or other proprietary material.

■ **Corruption:**

  ■ *Misuse of customer data.* Personnel inside or outside the organization can obtain employee or customer data and use the information to obtain credit or for other fraudulent purposes.

Important: Cyber fraudsters do not even have to leave their homes to commit fraud, as they can route communications through local phone companies, long-distance carriers, Internet service providers, and wireless and satellite networks.

Lesson for All

To prevent the increasingly numerous frauds spawned by the information age, management must know its vulnerabilities and be able to mitigate risk in a cost-effective manner. Therefore, IT risk should be *directly* included in the organization's overall fraud risk assessment . . . and resulting preventive controls.

White-Collar Crime Fighter source. *Managing the Business Risk of Fraud: A Practical Guide,* available from the AICPA, the IIA, or the ACFE.

Resources

For further information on detecting and preventing fraud:

The Accounts Payable Network, www.tapn.com

American Bankers Association (ABA), www.aba.com

American Institute of Certified Public Accountants (AICPA), www.aicpa.org

Association for Financial Professionals, www.afp.org

Association of Certified Fraud Examiners (ACFE), www.acfe.com

AuditNet, www.auditnet.org

BankersOnline.com, www.bankersonline.com

BankInfoSecurity.com, www.bankinforsecurity.com

Deloitte Forensic Center, www.deloitte.com/dtt/section_node/0,1042,sid%253D1 40674,00.html

Ethics Resource Center, www.ethics.org

Federal Bureau of Investigation, White-Collar Crime Division, www.fbi.gov/white collarcrime.htm

Federal Trade Commission, www.ftc.gov/bcp/menus/business/fraud.shtm

FraudAware, www.fraudaware.com

High-Tech Crime Investigation Association, www.htcia.org

Identity Theft Resource Center, www.idtheftcenter.org

Institute of Internal Auditors, www.theiia.org

Merchant 911, www.merchant911.org

Mortgage Fraud Reporter, www.mortgagefraud.org

NACHA, The Electronic Payments Association, www.nacha.org

National Association of Forensic Accountants, www.nafanet.com

National Association of Purchasing Card Professionals, www.napcp.org

National Bank Anti-Fraud Resource Center Banker Information, www.occ.treas .gov/AntiFraudBankers.htm

Securities and Exchange Commission, www.sec.gov

U.S. Comptroller of the Currency, www.occ.gov

White-Collar Crime Fighter, www.wccfighter.com

Notes

▶ Preface

1. Deepa Sarkar of the Cornell Law School Securities Law Clinic. Published by Wex, a collaboratively-created, public-access law dictionary and encyclopedia. It is sponsored and hosted by the Legal Information Institute at the Cornell Law School. http://topics.law.cornell.edu/wex.

▶ Chapter 1

1. Association of Certified Fraud Examiners (ACFE), *2008 Report to the Nation on Occupational Fraud and Abuse.*
2. Ibid.
3. Ibid.
4. Ibid.
5. *KPMG 2008–2009 Integrity Survey,* p. 11.
6. ACFE, 2008 Report.
7. *Ten Things about the Consequences of Financial Statement Fraud. A Look at Some of the Adverse Consequences Companies Have Experienced,* Deloitte Forensic Center, 2008 p. 6. Available at: *www.deloitte.com/dtt/cda/doc/content/ us_dfc_ttafsfconsequences_26112008(2).pdf.*
8. ACFE, 2008 Report.
9. Ken Yormark and Pam Verick Stone, "The Current State of Corporate Fraud Risk Management (FRM),) *Metropolitan Corporate Counsel* (March 2008): 28.
10. Economist Intelligence Unit.
11. *Global Fraud Report, Annual Edition 2008/2009,* Kroll Inc., p. 10.
12. Ibid.
13. Ibid.
14. *Eleventh Periodic Mortgage Fraud Case Report to Mortgage Bankers Association* by Asset Research Institute (MARI), p. 5, www.marisolutions.com/pdfs/mba/ mortgage-fraud-report-11th.pdf.

▶ Chapter 2

1. Donald R. Cressey, *Other People's Money* (Glencoe, IL: Free Press,1953), p. 3.

► **Chapter 3**

1. Tommie Singleton, PhD, Aaron J. Singleton, G. Jack Bologna, Robert J. Lindquist, *Fraud Auditing and Forensic Accounting* (Hoboken, N.J.: John Wiley & Sons, 2006), p. 116.

2. Association for Financial Professionals (AFP), *2008 AFP Payments Fraud and Control Survey*, www.afponline.org/pub/pdf/2008Payments FraudandContolSurvey.pdf p. 15.

3. Ibid., p. 15.

4. American National Standards Institute (www.ansi.org) and the Internet Security Alliance (www.isalliance.org), *The Financial Impact of Cyber Risk: 50 Questions Every CFO Should Ask*, http://webstore.ansi.org/cybersecurity .aspx p.15.

5. AFP, "2008 AFP Payments Fraud and Control Survey," p.19.

6. "Fraud Examination," Course at NorthWest Arkansas Community College taught by Sharon L. Curry, CFE, Wal-Mart Stores, Inc., www.nwacc.edu/aca-demics/criminaljustice/documents/Chapter1fraudexamination.pdf.

7. Office of the Comptroller of the Currency, *Check Fraud: A Guide to Avoiding Losses*,. p. 3. www.occ.treas.gov/chckfrd/chckfrd.pdf.

8. Karen Furst and Daniel E. Nolle, "What's Your Risk with the Growing Use of ACH Payments?" *OCC Quarterly Journal* (December 2005): 26.

9. NACHA data cited in 2007 *AFP Payments Fraud Survey Report of Survey Results*, p. 10. www.afponline.org/pub/pdf/2007PaymentsFraudSurvey.pdf.

10. Ibid.

11. Association of Certified Fraud Examiners, *2008 Report to the Nation on Occupational Fraud and Abuse*, p. 13.

12. Eric Cole, PhD, chief scientist for Lockheed Martin Information Technology, and coauthor of *Insider Threat: Protecting the Enterprise from Sabotage, Spying and Theft*, Syngress Publishing Inc., www.syngress.com.

13. Bruce Dubinstky and Christine Warner, "Uncovering Accounts Payable Fraud Using Fuzzy Matching Logic," *Business Credit* (March 2008).

14. *Purchasing/Payable Fraud,* white paper by Lowers & Associates, Loss Prevention Consultants (www.lowersrisk.com).

15. *Proactive Procurement Fraud Prevention Model,* by Craige Greene, CFE, CPA/ CFF, MCJ, Partner, McGovern & Greene LLP, Certified Public Accountants and Consultants, Chicago, www.mcgoverngreene.com.

16. AFP, 2008 *AFP Payments Fraud and Control Survey*, p. 5.

► **Chapter 4**

1. *United States v. Thomas Coughlin,* 2:06-cr-20005-RTD (W.D. Ark. 2008).

2. Transparency International, "Business Principles for Countering Bribery. An Initiative of Transparency International and Social Accountability International," p. 7, www.transparency.org/content/download/561/3429/file/ BPCBfinal.pdf.

3. Joseph T. Wells, *Corporate Fraud Handbook* (Hoboken, N.J.: John Wiley & Sons, 2006), p. 287.

4. *Fraud Examiners Manual*, 3rd ed. (Austin, Tex.: Association of Certified Fraud Examiner, 2001), pp. 2.201–2.207.

5. Statement of Offense in *United States v. Siemens Aktiengesellschaft*, U.S. District Court, Washington DC, www.usdoj.gov/opa/documents/siemens-agstmt-offense .pdf.

6. U.S. Department of Justice, www.usdoj.gov, Securities and Exchange Commission, www.sec.gov.

7. Project on Government Oversight (POGO), www.pogo.org.

8. Wells, *Corporate Fraud Handbook*, p. 328.

9. Vicky B. Heiman-Hoffman, Kimberly P. Morgan, and James M. Patton, "The Warning Signs of Fraudulent Financial Reporting," *Journal of Accountancy* 182 (1996).

10. Association of Certified Fraud Examiners, American Institute of Certified Public Accountants, and Institute of Internal Auditors, *Managing the Business Risk of Fraud: A Practical Guide*, 2008, p. 15.

11. Association of Certified Fraud Examiners 2008 *Report to the Nation on Occupational Fraud and Abuse*, p. 18.

12. Tommie W. Singleton, Aaron J. Singleton, G. Jack Bologna, and Robert J. Lindquist, *Fraud Auditing and Forensic Accounting*, 3rd ed. (Hoboken, N.J.: John Wiley & Sons, 2006), p. 180.

13. "White-Collar Crime 101 LLC," *White-Collar Crime Fighter*, (Ridgefield, CT), 10 no. 7.

▶ **Chapter 5**

1. *2007 Annual Study: U.S. Cost of a Data Breach: Understanding Financial Impact, Customer Turnover, and Preventive Solutions*, survey conducted by The Ponemon Institute, a research organization "dedicated to advancing ethical information and privacy management practices in business and government." It was founded by Larry Ponemon PhD, also a founding member of the Unisys Security Leadership Institute and an adjunct professor of Ethics & Privacy at Carnegie Mellon University's CIO Institute. For the full report, visit www.ponemon.org.

2. National Retail Federation's third annual Return Fraud Survey, 2008, www .nrf.com/modules.php?name=News&op=viewlive&sp_id=600

3. *CyberSource 10th Annual Online Fraud Report*, www.cybersource.com/cgi-bin/ resource_center/resources.cgi.

▶ **Chapter 6**

1. American Institute of Certified Public Accountants, *Statement on Auditing Standards (SAS) No. 99, Consideration of Fraud in a Financial Statement Audit*, p. 25.

2. Ibid.

3. American Institute of Certified Public Accountants, Institute of Internal Auditors, Association of Certified Fraud Examiners, *Managing the Business Risk of Fraud: A Practical Guide*, 2008 p. 6.

4. Ibid., p. 22.

5. Jonny Frank, *Deeper & Broader: Performing Fraud & Reputation Risk Assessments* (Institute of Internal Auditors, 2004).

6. Ibid.

7. Leonard Vona, *Fraud Risk Assessment, Building a Fraud Audit Program* (Hoboken, N.J.: John Wiley & Sons, 2008).

8. Nidhi Gupta, CPA, CFE, CIA, CAMS Director, BDO Consulting, a division of BDO Seidman, LLP, writing in *White-Collar Crime Fighter*, "The Roles of the Board and Management in Fraud Risk Assessments," (November 2008): 3.

▶ Chapter 7

1. Thomas W. Golden, Steven L. Skalak and Mona M. Clayton, *A Guide to Forensic Accounting Investigation* (PricewaterhouseCoopers LLP, New York, 2006), p. 179.

2. Ibid., p. 129.

3. American Institute of Certified Public Accountants, *Statement on Auditing Standards (SAS) No. 99, Consideration of Fraud in a Financial Statement Audit* and International Auditing and Assurance Standards Board of the International Federal of Accountants, *International Standard on Auditing (ISA) 240.*

4. Joseph T. Wells, *Corporate Fraud Handbook* (Hoboken, N.J.: John Wiley & Sons, 2006), pp. 390–392.

5. Martin T. Biegelman, Joel T. Bartow, *Executive Roadmap to Fraud Prevention and Internal Control: Creating a Culture of Compliance* (Hoboken: N.J.: John Wiley & Sons, 2006).

6. Ibid. p. 254–263.

▶ Chapter 8

1. Association of Certified Fraud Examiners, American Institute of Certified Public Accountants, and Institute of Internal Auditors, *Managing the Business Risk of Fraud: A Practical Guide*, p. 15.

2. American Institute of Certified Public Accountants, *Statement of Auditing Standards No. 99, Consideration of Fraud in a Financial Statement Audit*, p. 16.

3. Ibid. p. 75.

4. Ibid.

5. Ibid., pp. 24–25.
6. Ibid., pp. 26–27.
7. CCH, Inc., *Managing the Business Risk of Fraud, SAS 99,* author interviews with experienced forensic auditors.
8. Steve Albrecht, Conan C. Albrecht, and Chad O. Albrecht, *Fraud Examination,* 2nd ed. (Mason, OH, Thomson-South-Western, 2006), p. 164.

Glossary

A

accounts payable fraud Any fraud that impacts an organization's payments or disbursements, processes, and procedures. These may include check theft, check forgery, setting up sham vendors, vendor-perpetrated fraud, a variety of billing schemes, and ACH frauds.

asset misappropriation This type of fraud includes skimming revenues, stealing confidential customer data from company computers, check forgery, and payroll fraud.

B

bid rigging The illegal act of manipulating the competitive bidding process to ensure that a preferred vendor or contractor receives a contract—usually in exchange for a kickback or bribe.

bribery Money, a favor, or something else of value promised to, given to, or taken from an individual or organization in an attempt to sway decisions, such as the choice of vendor.

C

check fraud A category of schemes including theft of blank organization checks, forging endorsements, forging signatures, counterfeiting, intercepting mailed checks, and so on.

collusion Fraud committed by two perpetrators—usually one who works for the target organization and the other a dishonest outsider such as a vendor or customer.

computer fraud The deliberate unauthorized access, distribution, abuse, or alteration of electronic data—usually for financial gain.

conflict of interest A situation in which an employee or manager with influence to affect business decisions has a direct or indirect interest in an entity that is in a position to receive business from the organization. For example, a purchasing manager of an organization has a duty to perform her work with loyalty to that employer, thus choosing sellers who offer the best products at the lowest prices, but might be tempted to have the organization buy products from, for example, the manager's sibling, that are not as good or as cheap.

corruption This type of fraud occurs when an employee—usually a manager—abuses his power in a business transaction to get money or favors illegally. Bribery and kickbacks are common forms of corruption.

cyber extortion Hacking into an organization's database(s) of confidential customer or employee information, stealing it, and threatening to release it on the Internet if the organization does not do what the extortionist demands.

D

denial of service attack An attack on a computer system or network that causes a loss of service to users. A network of computers is used to bombard and overwhelm another network of computers with the intention of causing the server to crash. A Distributed Denial of Service (DDoS) attack relies on brute force by using attacks from multiple computers. These attacks can be used to extort money from the businesses targeted.

detection Methods used by fraud examiners, employees, auditors, or law enforcement officials to discover red flags or hard evidence of potential or actual fraud. Detection can range from management's learning about fraud from an employee tip, to using a confidential informant to detect evidence of fraud, to auditors conducting a full-scale fraud audit to discover signs of fraud.

double billing A form of accounts payable fraud in which a dishonest vendor or insider submits a duplicate bill after submitting a legitimate one in the hope that the accounts payable controls will not notice the duplicate invoice and simply pay it.

E

employee-level fraud Any fraud committed against an organization by someone who works for that organization and who is not a supervisor, manager, or executive.

extortion The illegal use of legitimate or criminally-obtained authority or influence to demand money, information, property, or other concessions from the targeted victim.

F

firewall A system that can detect and prevent unauthorized access to or from an individual PC or computer network. Private or sensitive information is kept inside the firewall, which can stop certain messages (like those containing viruses) from entering a network if they do not meet the organization's security standards.

forgery Falsely and fraudulently making or altering a document (as a check).

fraud risk assessment The procedure conducted by auditors or fraud examiners to identify types of fraudulent schemes or scenarios that could occur at the organization due to inadequate internal controls or to specific motives of fraudsters.

fraudulent financial reporting The category of frauds involving intentional misrepresentation of the organization's financial performance or condition. These frauds typically include creating fictitious sales, concealing liabilities, falsifying inventory values, and so on.

financial statement fraud Remember Enron? Financial numbers games destroyed the company and cost thousands of employees their jobs and life savings.

G

ghost employee An employee in name only. A fraudulently added name to the organization's payroll records in order to generate fraudulent paychecks to the perpetrator—usually an internal payroll staffer or senior manager.

H

hacker An unauthorized computer system user who attempts to or gains access to an information system.

I

identity fraud Use of someone else's identity to facilitate fraud. This usually involves the use of stolen or forged identity documents, such as a driver's license or Social Security number, to obtain goods or services by deception. Such frauds include fraudulently opening bank accounts, applying for loans and applying for credit cards.

identity theft Theft of the identity of another person by stealing personal identifying information (PII) which includes Social Security number, driver's license number, date of birth, and bank account information.

internal controls Measures designed to prevent fraud. These can be numerous in large organizations where the potential opportunities for employees or outsiders to commit fraud are numerous. They are formulated to foil specific types of fraud at all levels of the organization—entity level, department level, and process level.

inventory shrinkage A combination of employee theft, shoplifting, vendor fraud, and administrative error.

K

kickback An illegal payment by a seller to a purchasing agent as compensation for awarding the seller a piece of business.

M

mortgage fraud Any attempt by an applicant to obtain a mortgage by submitting false details about income, employment, or any bogus information supplied in support of a mortgage by mortgage brokers, appraisers, attorneys, or underwriters.

P

phishing Pronounced "fishing," the act of sending e-mail messages to multiple computer users, falsely claiming to be a legitimate enterprise, in an attempt to scam the user into surrendering private information that will be used for identity theft. The e-mail directs users to visit a fraudulent Website, where they are asked to update personal information, such as passwords and credit card, Social Security number, and bank account numbers, that the legitimate organization already has.

R

return fraud In retailing, when a customer asks for a refund for returning a stolen item or requests a refund for merchandise that was purchased and then returned to the store with the receipt and bringing identical items to the customer service desk for a refund.

S

Sarbanes-Oxley Act This law was signed by President George W. Bush in 2002 in response to the Enron debacle and other major corporate frauds. It put into place tough rules and regulations about what company auditors and top executives can and cannot do when it comes to managing the company's financial statements and reports. One of the Act's main requirements is that all public company Chief Executive Officers, and Chief Financial Officers must now certify all financial statements, taking responsibility for the accuracy of these statements. If it is later found that the statements covered up illegal financial activity, these executives can be charged with criminal activity.

T

Trojan horse A piece of software that, when loaded onto your company via e-mail or downloading Internet files, allows a hacker to take control of your PC behind your back. A Trojan infection can allow total remote access to your computer by a cyber criminal.

W

worm A software program created by a hacker that copies itself from machine to machine across network connections, usually crippling networks and information systems as it spreads.

About the Author

Peter Goldmann is president of White-Collar Crime 101 LLC, the publisher of *White-Collar Crime Fighter,* a monthly newsletter for internal auditors, controllers, corporate counsel, financial operations managers, and fraud investigators.

Peter has published *White-Collar Crime Fighter* since 1998 and has interviewed hundreds of fraud investigators, forensic accountants, white-collar crime attorneys, ex-convicts, and auditors.

In addition, White-Collar Crime 101 has developed the leading employee fraud awareness training program, *FraudAware.* This is a user-friendly workshop and E-learning training tool designed to educate employees at all levels in how to detect, prevent and report incidents of fraud or suspicious conduct.

The course, which is customized for individual corporate, non-profit, and government agency clients, reinforces companies' whistleblowing programs, by enabling employees to detect fraudulent activity that can then be reported to supervisors or managers or by using the organization's confidential hotline.

Peter has 25 years of experience as a business journalist and trainer, having launched, edited, and published numerous business trade periodicals covering small business, international trade, management strategy, banking, and personal finance. He is a member of the Editorial Advisory Committee of the Association of Certified Fraud Examiners (ACFE) as well as an active member of the Institute of Internal Auditors, the High-Tech Crime Investigation Association and InfraGard.

He is a regular columnist for the ACFE's newsletter, *The Fraud Examiner* and is a frequent contributor to other leading industry publications on anti-fraud topics. He has appeared on *The Wall Street Journal This Morning,* Fox Business News, *The New York Times* and *Internal Auditor* magazine.

He can be reached at pgoldmann@wccfighter.com.

Index